The GOOD CHILD Guide

2nd Edition

Dr. Noel Swanson

The GOOD CHILD Guide
Putting an End to Bad Behavior
2nd Edition

ISBN 978-0-9783686-0-9

© Noel Swanson, 2000, 2007
Cartoon illustrations by Harry Venning

Noel Swanson has asserted his moral right to be identified as the author of this work in accordance with the Copyright, Design and Patents Act 1988, UK

All rights reserved. No part of this publication may be reproduced, stored in a retrieval system, or transmitted, in any form or by any means, without prior permission in writing from the publisher.

This manual is provided in good faith as educational information only. It should not be relied upon as medical or psychological advice, and no liability can be accepted for any harm or damages caused by the use or misuse of the information provided. If you need personalized advice for your own unique situation, please consult a qualified professional.

Published by
Allegretto Publishing Ltd.
50 Southshore Drive
Brooks, AB T1R 1M4
Canada

www.good-child-guide.com

TABLE OF CONTENTS

INTRODUCTION 7

CHAPTER 1

WHY DO THEY DO WHAT THEY DO? 11

Motivation - The Key Factor 13
    People Do What They Want To Do 13
    All behaviors have consequences 13
    Children are Gamblers 15
    Children's Tactics For Getting What They Want 17
    It Gets Worse Before It Gets Better 18
    Changing Behaviors 20

Temperament, Emotions, and other Internal Factors 21
    Understanding Temperaments 21
    The Internal Switch 23
    Sleep, Food and Warmth 24
    Self-Confidence, Fear of Failure, and Learned Helplessness 24
    Fear and Anxiety 27
    Chronic Stress 27
    Security and Being Noticed 28
    Anger and Resentment 29
    The Emotional Bank Account 29
    Paying off the Mortgage 30
    People Still Do What They Want To Do 31

Power Struggles and Manipulation 33

CHAPTER 2

PUTTING YOURSELF BACK IN CHARGE 37

The New Improved YOU 39
    The Repeating, Threatening Parent 39
        1)   Say what you mean, and mean what you say. 40
        2)   Talk with a firm but quiet voice. 41
        3)   Expect First Time Obedience. 41
        4)   Follow up with ACTION. 41
    Harsh, Strict or Firm? 41
    The Carrot and The Stick 43
    Reward Mode vs. Punishment Mode 44
    Who Owns The Success? 45
    The Informal Checks And Balances Of Home Life 46

Dr. Noel Swanson

Getting Started 47
    Recognize the Enemy 47
    Think Ahead 48
    Have A United Front. 49
    Get Some Support 49
    Walk Your Talk 49
    Reset Your Expectations And Clear The Slate 50
    Where Do You Start? 51

CHAPTER 3

STOPPING BAD BEHAVIORS 55

Three Counts and You're Out! 57
    1-2-3-Magic! 57
    Time-Out 61
    Rules for Time-Out 62
    Variations on Time-Out 64
    The 5-Minute Work Chore 65
    Loss of Privileges 65
    Avoiding Sudden Death 66
    Other Tactics 67
        The Broken Record 67
        Ignoring 67
        Grounding 68
        Spanking 69

More Serious "Crimes" 70
    Bad Morals, Disobedience and Naughtiness 71

Lying 74

Stealing 77

CHAPTER 4

STARTING GOOD BEHAVIORS 81

Seven Strategies 83

Responsibility 85
    What is Responsibility? 86
    Natural Consequences 87
    Logical Consequences 88

Charting 90
    Common Questions 94
    Why isn't it working? 94

Variations on Charting 95
Progressive Privileges 96
Contracts 96
Pocket Money 97

Payment **98**

Make it a Game! **99**

Praise and Compliments **102**
Special Treats and Rewards 103

CHAPTER 5

SPECIFIC PROBLEM BEHAVIORS **105**

How to Analyze a Specific Behavior **107**

Mornings **111**

School Refusal And Separation Anxiety **114**

Homework **116**

Bedtimes **118**
Midnight Wakenings 120
Night Terrors, Nightmares, and Sleep Walking 121
Early Mornings 122

I'm Bored! **123**

Attention Deficit Hyperactivity Disorder **124**

CHAPTER 6

AS TIME GOES BY **127**

How Are You Doing? **129**
The Family Meeting 129
Slipping Back 131
They Are Getting Older 131

Final Words **133**

CHAPTER 7

APPENDICES **135**

Suggestions for Rewards 137

Things to Do When You Are Bored 138

Agenda for Family Conference 139

The 6 A's of Apology 140

The Deal 141

INTRODUCTION

Parenting has to be the toughest job on Earth. For most of us it comes at a time when we have little experience of life, no money, and are just trying to establish ourselves in a job or career. On top of that we are trying to work out just what it means to be living with a relatively new spouse or partner. For some of us, parenthood is quite unexpected and perhaps unwanted, forcing us out of a job or education, and leaving us stranded without a supportive partner, decent accommodation, or a reasonable income.

At first it is all very new, but also reasonably straightforward – feed, change diapers, put to bed. But as time goes by, it gets more complicated. Often it may seem to be a never-ending cycle of guilt, worry, stress and broken nights. Of course there are the occasional moments of joy – the first smile, the first step, the Christmas concert, looking in on the cute little angels as they lie fast asleep in bed – but sometimes it seems that these are awfully small rewards for all the hassle (and expense) of trying to raise them.

For some of us, this may then be further complicated by separation or divorce, money problems, or chronic illness or disability. Certainly, society seems to be heaping more and more stress on to families and the children themselves. There seem to be ever more dangers lurking around, waiting to entice our children into sex, drugs or depression, to name but a few.

Behavior problems among children are on the increase. This is a reflection of our increasingly complex and frantic society. It is harder to be a parent today than it was even just a generation ago. Therefore today's parents need skills and strategies to help them create a home in which their children can grow up to be mature, responsible, loving adults who are a credit to their families and to society.

This manual will teach you those strategies. If you are having problems in controlling the behavior of your children, if the fun (what's that?) seems to have gone and family life seems to be all work, or if you simply want to learn to be the best parent that you can, this is the manual for you.

The strategies covered in this manual are primarily targeted at children aged five to twelve, but the principles apply to all children (and even adults), and many parents have found the manual to be very helpful with children aged from as little as 17 months right up to 17 years. Furthermore, everything in here is applicable to children of all abilities and personalities, including those with specific disorders such as Attention Deficit Hyperactivity Disorder (ADHD) and dyslexia.

Dr. Noel Swanson

The principles that form the foundations of this manual are based on my experience of twenty years as an adult, and then child and adolescent, psychiatrist in three countries (Britain, Canada, and Belize), and as a parent of two children, one of whom has Asperger's Syndrome. The manual also benefits from my experience of over seven years developing and running leadership-training seminars with not-for-profit organizations in the developing world. Here you will find detailed instructions that will lead you step by step through some strategies that will very quickly help you to correct common behavior problems such as disobedience, defiance and irresponsibility. If you are in a hurry, you can turn straight to those chapters and start to use them today.

However, every child is different, as is every parent, and so in here you will also learn the enduring principles of parenting that will enable you to adapt and create strategies so that they become tailor-made for your own situation and your own family's values and goals.

Since parenting is a long-term job, it would serve us well to consider what the long-term goals are. At times it seems to be as much as we can do to make it from one day to the next. The danger is that we may choose the easy route rather than the most beneficial route. For example, it is often much easier to sit children down in front of the TV than for us to create the space and time to do something more constructive with them. Unless we consider our ultimate aims and objectives as parents, the way in which we parent our children will be more determined by the influences of society – work pressures, school, TV, magazines, friends – than by us.

This need not be the case. By carefully considering your aims for the future, you can determine what skills, abilities and attitudes your children will need to have, if they are to be better equipped to face this world than we were as youngsters. To then put this into practice may take some commitment, work and sacrifice, but in fact you will be pleasantly surprised at how easy it actually is. Your day-to-day family life will be enhanced, and fun will begin to reappear. You will also have the satisfaction of knowing that you have done all that you humanly could to provide your children with the best start to life that they could have.

Most people who pick up a book on parenting do so because they are having some specific difficulties, usually with behavior. The goal, therefore, is to be as practical as possible so that you can quickly start to see results. Even so, it is important to lay down some basic groundwork so that you can understand why it is that things are not working so well at present and the basic principles for starting to do things differently. These first couple of chapters are perhaps the most difficult ones. But please, persevere with them, and soon you will be able to start putting them into practice. Too often people try a new behavioral system, but then run into difficulties because they do not really understand why it is not working for them. Hopefully Chapter 1 will prevent that difficulty.

Chapter 2 then gets more practical, looking at how to get out of Repeating, Threatening Parent mode and into reward mode. These basic principles are then examined in even more detail as we look at how to stop bad behavior and start good behavior, step by step. These strategies have been well proven in hundreds of thousands of homes and, if carefully followed, will undoubtedly also prove effective in your home. Just do as the manual says, and before too long the fun should start creeping back into family life.

Finally, we look at some very common problems, including morning, bedtimes, lying and stealing. Once again the basic principles are used to develop some detailed suggestions on how to tackle them. You will also learn how to analyze other problem behaviors so that you can design your own corrective strategies. At this stage, you will no longer be dependent on detailed instructions and will actually be able to work out your own solutions to your own particular challenges.

Included in all of this are strategies to develop character, morals, respect, love and forgiveness.

In the final analysis, you are not just a parent; you are a person. As you read this manual, you may also discover ways in which you yourself can grow and mature even further as a person. Life is not just a series of events, but a journey. On this journey you can either blindly stumble about, or you can open your eyes and try to look where you are going. By buying this manual you have already decided that you cannot stumble blindly any longer. My hope is that you will come to understand yourself better, and as a result you will move a little further along on the journey to wholeness and maturity.

In writing this manual I have had to deal with the tricky issue of gender. Although more boys than girls have behavior problems, both need effective parenting. Since the English language does not have gender-inclusive words to cover both him and her, he and she, I have chosen to alternate the use of these pronouns. In addition, I have also used various boys' and girls' names to better illustrate the points. These are not, of course, the names of any particular real-life children, nor are they to be taken to suggest that children with those names are more likely to have problems than other children. So if, by chance, I have picked a name that happens to be the name of your child – I am not picking on you! Honestly!

The same problem arises in addressing you, the parents. You may or may not be married. To cover all eventualities, I have chosen to use the rather inadequate word 'partner' to include spouse, husband, wife, boyfriend or girlfriend. I realize this is far from ideal, and I hope you will not be too irritated by the term. Of course you may not have a partner at all at present. All is not lost! If being a parent is tough, being a single parent is in a whole new dimension. But it can be done successfully, and this manual will be as applicable to you as to any other parent.

No one ever said that parenting would be easy. In making the decision to be the best parent that you can for your children, instead of just leaving it to fate, you may even be making it a bit harder! My hope is that this manual will ease your task by providing strategies that work and principles that will carry you through the years ahead. I also hope that this manual will help you and your family to have more fun and to feel more fulfilled. After all, life isn't supposed to be all work and no play!

This manual is dedicated to you and to every other parent who has made the commitment to be the best parent they can.

Dr. Noel Swanson

CHAPTER 1

WHY DO THEY DO WHAT THEY DO?

CHAPTER 1 - 1

Motivation - The Key Factor

People Do What They Want To Do

If you are like most parents, there will be times when you scratch your head and wonder, 'Why on Earth do they keep doing these things?' The answer to this question is surprisingly simple – they do what they do because they want to!

This might sound a very silly thing to say, but it is absolutely true. People do what they want to do – and that applies to me, to you, to your partner, and to your children.

Of course it is not really quite that simple, but understanding this principle is the key to bringing order, peace and even fun back into your home. Once you fully understand this principle, and once you learn to apply it to your life and your family's life, you will be well on the way to success. So let's look at it in detail.

As we go through life, we are constantly faced with choices. At any particular time there are a number of things that we could do, and out of these various options there are certain actions, or behaviors, that we actually choose. Sometimes these choices are trivial – shall I sit on this chair or that chair, shall I get out of bed now, or in five minutes' time? At other times the choices are more serious – shall I race through the red traffic light? Shall I cheat on my tax return? Sometimes we think long and hard about the choices we make, for example, when planning to move house or change career. At other times our decisions are so quick and so spontaneous that we hardly even know that we are making them, such as when we 'automatically' choose to brush our teeth at night, or when we choose to scratch our head because it is itching.

But whatever behavior is chosen, the process of choosing that behavior is the same. It is based on the very simple principle: 'What's in it for me?' What we do is weigh up the pros and cons of behavior A compared to behavior B and then choose the one that seems to offer the greatest gain or the least pain. In other words, we consider the consequences of the behaviors.

All behaviors have consequences

Consequences come in all sorts of different shapes and sizes: some trivial, some monumental, some good, some bad, some immediate, and some in the distant future. Some consequences will be very obvious to us as we make our choices, whereas we may

Dr. Noel Swanson

not know about others for many years to come. As we make our choices, we may think long and hard about all the possible consequences, or we may just jump into the first behavior we think of as it seems to offer some obvious benefit.

Now, at this point you may be objecting: 'But I don't want to pay my taxes, so how can you say that I am doing it because I want to?' Well, actually you do want to, because what you are doing is weighing up the pros and cons. On balance, you have decided that the pain of paying is less than the pain of going to jail. Given the limitations of the circumstances in which you find yourself, you prefer (i.e. want) to pay your taxes. The same applies to other unpleasant situations in which the circumstances force us to choose between various options that are all 'painful' in some way.

All consequences can, therefore, be divided into three groups: rewards, punishments, and those that can be deemed neutral.

Very simply, a *reward* is any consequence that **increases** the likelihood or frequency of the associated behavior. It reinforces the behavior. A *punishment* is any consequence that **decreases** the likelihood or frequency of a particular behavior.

Neutral consequences have no effect on the frequency or likelihood of the behaviors.

Note this very carefully: rewards or punishments are **any** consequences that change the frequency of behaviors. Furthermore, they are defined on the basis of how they affect behavior, not on whether people like or dislike the consequence. For example, if you want to get someone to pick up the telephone, the easiest way to do it is to make the telephone ring. The ringing telephone confronts people with a choice: to pick it up or not pick it up. The consequence of not picking it up is that the ringing will continue, and for most people this produces an internal state of tension. To relieve the tension, they pick up the phone. The ringing then stops. In this case, the action of picking up the phone has been rewarded by the decrease in tension, as well as the satisfaction of finding out who is calling.

The consequences that occur outside of us as a result of our behaviors, the rewards and punishments, motivate us to act this way or that. They can therefore be described as **external motivators**. These include such obvious things as the gain or loss of money, privileges, freedom, and physical, sexual, or emotional pleasure or pain - consequences caused by our environment or the people we relate to. But external motivators also include such intangibles as social approval or ostracism, attention, or seeing someone else become happy or sad.

However, one man's meat is another man's poison. What may be a very rewarding consequence for one person may be a major punishment for another. For example, in some situations or for some people, being noticed by a large crowd of people may be a wonderful reward and incentive for certain behaviors, whereas on a different occasion or for other people, it might prove to be very embarrassing and so a significant disincentive or punishment. For children, getting a parent's attention is highly rewarding. This is true even when the attention includes shouting. Moreover, getting Mom or Dad all worked up and upset may also be quite stimulating and exciting. If that is so, it is easy to see how

The GOOD CHILD Guide

getting into a fight with Mom can be much more rewarding than playing quietly and being ignored by her.

What is it that determines whether a particular consequence acts as a reward or a punishment for us? This largely depends on a number of internal factors – for example, our personality and temperament, mood and emotions. In addition, our principles and morals, self-confidence and security, and our basic needs for food, warmth, sex, and so on will further affect how much these external consequences motivate us. Some of these internal states are long-term, some change by the minute, but all are vitally important in modifying how we will respond to the world around us at any one time. We will discuss these factors in more detail in the next section.

What is important is this: if your child is doing something, whatever it is, it is because there is some reward to be gained or some pain (punishment) to be avoided. In other words, **he is doing it because it pays!** You may not understand how it pays. You may feel that it cannot possibly pay, and that there is absolutely nothing that could be gained from this behavior. But you would be wrong. The very fact that the behavior is happening means it must be paying off – otherwise he wouldn't do it.

That's it! Now you know what makes people tick and why they do what they do – well, almost. There are a few other factors that we need to consider, but maybe it's time to look at those little angels of yours; why do they do what they do?

Children are Gamblers

'Mom, can I have a cookie?'

'No, we are having supper in a minute.'

'Aw, Muuuuuuum . . . I need a cookie.'

'No, I told you, not until after supper!'

'Go on, Mom, just one . . .'

What happens next? How long does the 'discussion' continue – five minutes, ten minutes? Or does it develop into a full-blown shouting match with tears and foot stamping? How does it end? Does Mom give in? Does little Katie get her cookie?

I am frequently asked by frustrated parents why scenes like this are repeated so often. Of course the item under discussion can be almost anything - treats, TV time, later bedtime, extra favors - but the format never changes. So what happens here? Surely children don't enjoy being shouted at?

This is when it is important to remember that children are like gamblers. Think of the slot machines. The punter comes along and puts a coin in the machine and hopes to win. If he does not win, then in goes another coin, followed by another, and another. Sometimes he wins, but most of the time he does not.

Dr. Noel Swanson

Why does the gambler keep playing the machine even when he doesn't win? According to the discussion above, isn't the loss of his coin a punishment that should decrease the frequency of his behavior? The answer is simple, of course. He plays because he hopes to win, and for him the chance of winning a big prize is a greater motivator than the risk of losing smaller amounts. Furthermore, at irregular intervals the machine does actually pay out, and this of course reinforces the gambling behavior. So you can see that it is not necessary for the reward to happen every time in order to reinforce the behavior. In fact, intermittent reward schedules like this are actually much more effective in keeping a certain behavior going.

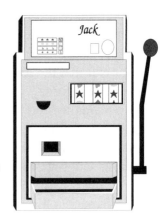

Let's look at our gambler again. But this time, let us assume that the machine has broken down. It can still be played, but it no longer pays out. The punter does not know this, and so in goes the coin. This time he does not win. But no matter, he knows that he does not win every time. Perhaps the next time . . . and in goes another coin, and then another, and another, and another . . .

After about two weeks of playing this machine and not winning, our friend starts to get suspicious. He asks a few of his friends if they have won anything on this machine recently. Eventually, since neither he nor his friends have won anything for two weeks running, he finally concludes that there must be something wrong with the machine. He gives it a good kick in disgust and goes off to find one that does work.

Note that because the rewards were only intermittent, it took a full two weeks for the behavior (playing that particular machine) to stop. Had the machine paid out every single time (like a vending machine), then on the first occasion that it did not pay he would have been off to see the manager to complain!

Children are just like the gambler. Often when they do things, it is not because it pays off every time, but because it pays off sometimes.

Let's look at Katie and her quest for a cookie again. Katie is the gambler. You, as her parent, are the machine. She plays the game by asking for a cookie. You, the machine, refuse to pay out. 'Oh, well, didn't pay out that time', figures Katie, so she plays it again: 'Mom, I need a cookie!'. Maybe this time the machine will pay.

On most occasions this exchange probably ends with mother getting mad and sending Katie to her room. However, no doubt there are times when Mom is just too tired, or too hassled, or too busy, to argue. 'Oh, all right then, have a cookie! But mind it doesn't spoil your appetite!' And so, finally, the machine has paid out, and the behavior has been reinforced.

Why does the whining and arguing continue? Because sometimes it pays out. And when it doesn't? The worst thing that happens is that Mom gets cross and perhaps you are sent to your room.

In addition to this there is actually another reward that is operating here to reinforce this behavior: Mom's attention. All the time that Katie is engaged in the 'discussion', she is getting attention from Mom. It may not be the most positive attention, nor may it be her full attention, but it is attention, and that has to count for something.

Here is another example. This time it is little Johnny who is the culprit.

Food For Thought

Any Attention - even negative attention - can act as a reward

---

Johnny is sitting with his feet on the sofa, watching TV while eating chips. His coat and school bag are strewn across the floor. Dad passes him on the way to help Mom bring in the shopping.

'Johnny, get your feet off the sofa and go do your homework – and hang up your coat!'

Johnny blithely ignores him and carries on eating his chips, leaving crumbs everywhere.

As Dad comes in from the car, loaded up with potatoes, he shouts, 'Johnny, have you hung up your coat yet?'

Now, from past experience Johnny has learned that Dad does not really mean business yet. So he continues to ignore him. After each trip out to the car, Dad shouts another reminder. This is where the gamble comes in. Dad is pretty busy at this point, so there is quite a good chance that Dad will get distracted and forget about Johnny. But even if he does remember, and comes and chases after him, Johnny has still got away with an extra fifteen minutes of TV time! So what does he have to lose? It's worth the gamble.

Children's Tactics For Getting What They Want

Through numerous scenes like that, your children will have worked out a number of tactics that usually get them what they want. They are probably experts at them all, having had years of practice. These are the main ones:

Whining and persistent bugging

This is designed to wear you down until you give in. Like a pit bull terrier, they just do not let go and can keep up a persistent whine for days if necessary. Eventually you give in, if only for a quiet life. But what have you done? You have just paid out the jackpot, and rewarded the very behavior you are trying to stop.

Temper tantrums

With this one, the goal is to make such a scene, and to look so upset and distressed, that the poor parent has to do something to settle you down. The young ones are experts at this, but older ones can do it well too. It is wonderfully effective in public places, as most parents will do anything to avoid the embarrassment of appearing to have such an obviously ill-disciplined child. Pay-off time again!

Dr. Noel Swanson

Intimidation and threats

The (usually older) child starts shouting, swearing, throwing things, hitting you, or making it very clear that if you do not give him what he wants then something very bad is going to happen. Threatening to hurt you, your pets or your property are the common ones. Threats to run away or commit suicide are especially effective, as few parents are brave enough to call their bluff.

Guilt

The objective of this tactic is to make you realize what a rotten, mean, unfair parent you are. It usually begins with comments such as, 'I hate you, you are so mean!', accompanied by, 'If you loved me you would give it to me. Everyone else has it.' This is then followed by stomping up to the bedroom, slamming the door, and sulking for the rest of the day, or longer if need be. After a while you will reconsider your hasty and ridiculously unfair decision. After all, if everyone else has it, it cannot be that bad, surely? You would not want your precious little angel to feel unloved, would you?

This tactic works best when there are just the two of you in the home. This gives Mom or Dad the maximum opportunity to brood over it, without being able to make a reality check with the other parent.

The Bribe

This is a prime manipulation tactic (see the section on power struggles and manipulation later in the chapter). The older child promises to do something that you want him to do (homework, for example) in return for something that he wants. 'If you let me watch the football, then I'll do my homework straight afterwards.' Of course, once the football is over, there is no way that you will get him to keep his end of the bargain. Or it might be that he wants his pocket money early, before he has done his chores, as there is a special something that he just has to have right now. Don't fall for it – payment and rewards come after the work is done, not before.

Buttering Up

This is the opposite of the bribe. Suddenly she is all sweetness and light, offering to help with the dishes, putting things away, making you cups of tea. You are just thinking what a pleasant change this makes when she innocently asks you for that new computer game she has been on about for ages. How can you refuse? That would be so ungrateful when she has been so pleasant. Jackpot time! Then the next day she is back to her usual self.

You will no doubt recognize these various tactics from your own experience. Perhaps you even remember using them yourself when you were younger.

It Gets Worse Before It Gets Better

In this manual you will discover some powerful strategies that will change the way things work at home. You are going to get back in control of the house. The old, unwanted behaviors will no longer pay off, and instead, if the children want to get what they want, they will have to try some new, better, behaviors. In effect, all the old slot machines will be rigged so they no longer pay out, and a new set of machines will be installed.

The problem is that the children do not know that. You may have told them that this is how it is going to be, but they have heard it all before. Like the gambler, they will continue to play the old machines for another few weeks, expecting them to pay out, until they finally realize that all the old tactics just do not work any more.

Take a look at Katie again. This time she is after a new Barbie doll.

"Mom, when can I get that new Barbie?"

"Maybe for your birthday"

"But I want it now!"

"Sorry, you will have to wait."

At this point, Katie realizes that the machine has not paid out - she did not get her Barbie. So what does she do next? Does she meekly give in? Not on your life! First she will have a go at the old faithfuls:

"Aw, Muuuuum, that's months away. I need it now!" *(Whining, maybe combined with some pouting and foot stomping temper tantrum).*

"You don't expect me to play with old ones do you? I'm bored of them, I've had them ages." *(Poor little waif - what an uncaring mother she has).*

"Fine, don't give me anything then. You don't care. I'm going. If you loved me you would at least get me some toys to play with. I'm running away!" *(Threats and intimidation).*

Now, if Mom has learned her lessons, she will not be giving in to this. (Counting or ignoring are appropriate tactics here. We will cover these in detail later.) So what does Katie do? Give up? In your dreams. No, this is how Katie sees it:

She wants something. She is not getting it, despite using the regular tactics. She knows that the regular tactics normally work. So what is needed now is even more of the old tactics. If shouting is not working, then try shouting louder, or add in kicking, or punching, or throwing things, or threats, or suicide. Eventually, something should work. When it does, and Mom finally gives in to her, then she will have rewarded Katie's manipulation, making it even more likely to happen again next time.

As you can see, this manual will not provide you with an instant cure! Once you start using what you have learnt, life will probably get worse at first. Unless you are prepared for it, you may think that the new system is not working. Since things seem to be getting

Dr. Noel Swanson

worse rather than better, you give up. Bad decision. You have to stick with this until you get over the hump. After a few days of trying and failing, Katie will realize that the old tactics are not working anymore. They used to, but something seems to have changed. Eventually, she will realize that maybe she should try that 'please and thank you' routine that you keep going on about. Be warned, it may take some time to get there. So do not give up halfway or you will be worse off than ever.

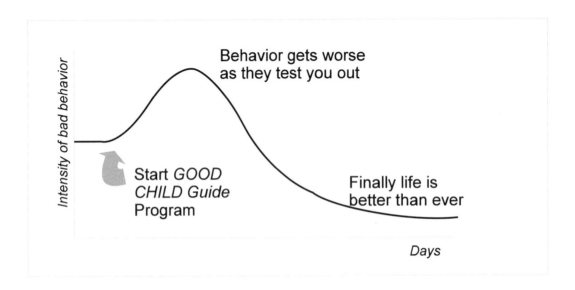

Changing Behaviors

By now, you will have started to figure out the basic principle for changing behaviors. If you want a behavior to stop, you will need to do three things:

1. Change the environment, so that the bad behavior no longer pays. That means you will need to work out how the current behavior is paying off and then find a way to stop those rewards.

2. Change the environment so that an alternative (good) behavior starts to pay off better.

3. Follow instructions 1 and 2 consistently and for long enough so that the bad behavior no longer seems worth the gamble and the good behavior becomes a much better bet.

We will of course look at this area in much more detail as we go on. But first, we need to understand some of the other factors that modify your child's behaviors.

CHAPTER 1 - 2

Temperament, Emotions, and other Internal Factors

In the last section we looked at how external consequences, the rewards and punishments in life, motivate your child. In this section we will see how this motivation is modified by the child's internal factors. The first of these is your child's inborn temperament.

Understanding Temperaments

Children do not come into the world as a blank sheet of paper waiting to be written on. Every child starts life with a different biological make-up. Different eye colors, different hair, different sizes, and also different temperaments.

By nature, some children are placid, whilst others are fidgety. Some are quiet and intense, whilst others are restless and always on the go. Some rush in where angels fear to tread, others think long and hard before doing anything. To a large extent these inborn temperamental characteristics will remain with the child throughout life.

Quite naturally, the child's temperament will affect his or her behavior. Some children seem to be naturally obedient and well behaved; others, born in the same family, seem to always come out fighting. If you have more than one child, you will already have noticed that they have very different personalities.

This is a very important point to remember. If your children are wonderfully behaved (why are you reading this manual?) then it may be because you are excellent, wonderful super parents. Or it may just be that you have been blessed with very easy children. If that is the case, then a word of advice: don't have any more! You might be in for a rude awakening with the next one!

But if (as is more likely, since you are still reading this manual), your little angels are, shall we say, a little less than angelic, then it may indeed be because you are rotten, awful, incompetent parents. (People have probably told you that already, haven't they?) Or it may be that you have been blessed with the challenge of raising some temperamentally very difficult children.

Do NOT fall into the trap of blaming yourselves. And, especially, do not allow others to judge you. After all, they do not know what your children are like. If they are to judge at all, what they need to be judging is not how good your kids are, but how much better or worse they are than they might have been with a different set of parents. Confused? Let's look at it this way:

Dr. Noel Swanson

Let's measure behavior on a scale of minus 10 to plus 10, with the average child being at the mid-point, which is zero (see diagram).

If your child is temperamentally very challenging, perhaps with a recognizable problem such as Attention Deficit Hyperactivity Disorder (ADHD) or Asperger's Syndrome, then your child might start out in life with a score of -8 (point A on the diagram).

But suppose that you are the perfect parents, and after seven years of hard, dedicated parenting, your child is behaving at a -3 level (point B). What will the neighbors be saying? Most likely they will look at the bad behavior and sadly shake their heads over the poor parents the child obviously has. And will you be agreeing with them? Or will you be able to recognize what a good job you have done? Getting him from -8 to -3 is no mean feat, and you should feel as proud as the parents who raise their average child from zero to +5. You have certainly done better than the poor parents whose easy, placid child started at +5 and now is at only +3.

Remember also that there are many other factors that affect your children – their schoolmates, their other relatives, the neighborhood they live in, the experiences, good and bad, that they encounter in life. Even if you are the best parent on Earth, you will not be able to protect them from some of the harm that others may do to them.

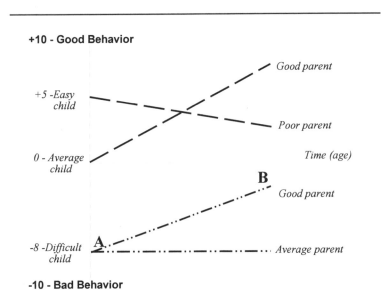

But we cannot let you off the hook completely! None of us is perfect, and you, like me, can still make some improvements in your parenting skills. The goal here is to be as honest in your self-assessment as you can, not in order to apportion blame, but so that you can identify as accurately as possible your strengths and weakness. Then you can enhance the former, and improve or compensate for the latter.

There is no point in beating yourself over the head with guilt and anguish about what a failure you are as a parent. Even if it is true, doing so will actually prevent you from becoming a better one. But if things are not going well at home, you cannot blame the child either. After all, no matter how difficult your child is, it is still your job as the parent to try to figure out how best to improve things, and this will never happen if you start seeing your child as the enemy.

Be honest. Look at the past. See what you have done well and what has not gone so well. Remember to take into account the child's temperament. Then determine to yourself that you will improve upon what you have done wrong, and reinforce what you have done right. After all, that is what you are expecting your child to do, isn't it?

The Internal Switch

By nature, some children are neat and tidy; others are total slobs. You go into one child's bedroom and it is like a show house. You go into the room of another, and you immediately trip over the K'nex model that is strewn over the floor. The first example (unless it is taken to an obsessive extreme) is a delight to any family, but what do we do about the second?

It is almost like there is a little switch inside the brain. For the tidy child, this switch is in the on position. Just put him in a messy room and he immediately starts to straighten it out, even if there is no (external) reward attached to it; the satisfaction of having everything in its place is reward enough.

The messy child does not see it that way at all. For her, the tidy switch is in the off position. The untidy child (or adult) will simply sit down in the mess and start reading her comic. She sees a messy room, and it means nothing to her. She sees a tidy room, and it also means nothing to her. Since she does not value tidiness in itself, why should she want to tidy up?

What we see here are two children placed in the same environment, with two different outcomes. The difference is of course that the child's internal state, in this case the tidiness temperament, has modified the meaning of the external consequences. For one, the clean room is a reward, for the other it means nothing. To the first one you can say, 'Tom, go tidy your room' and he thinks, 'What a good idea!' You say the same thing to the other, and she replies, 'What's in it for me?'

In the short-term, there is nothing we can do to change these internal motivations. However much you may shout, plead or argue, you will not turn an untidy child into a tidy one. All that you can do is to set up the external rewards and punishments so as to entice her to choose to clean up rather than to read comics. This reality is very frustrating to parents who have visions of their messy children growing up to be tramps living in a trash dump! It is, however, the crucial point: children do what they want to do, and the only way you can influence that is through the external environment. Bear in mind, though, that children do go through developmental phases, and so the same child might be very tidy at one age, and a disaster at another (just think of the average teenager!).

In the long-term, things do look a little more hopeful. The internal switches can be turned on or off over time. There are no guaranteed results, but establishing a regular, rewarding habit may, over time, change the setting of these switches.

Each child approaches every circumstance in his own unique way. Remember that this is not a deliberate, conscious process. The untidy child does not look at the mess and say to herself, 'This room is a mess, but it is not rewarding for me to clean it'; she does not even see that it is a mess. Similarly, some children are eager to please and to help, whilst others are much less aware of other people's needs. The former will willingly offer to help in the kitchen or to take out the trash. The others will have to be specifically asked. Each child modifies and interprets the external environment, including the gains and pains, in a different way. How boring it would be if they were all identical! But it does mean that you cannot expect the same behaviors from each. There really is no point in getting frustrated with Susan because she does not keep her room nice and tidy like Tom does. That is judging it from your perspective, not hers. As far as she is concerned, her room is just fine as it is.

This same principle applies to every other behavior: in each situation, the child has some of the switches on and some off.

But temperament is not the only thing that modifies the external motivators. It is the most enduring factor, but there are a host of other internal states that play a part. On the whole, however, most of these act as **de-motivators** rather than motivators. In other words, these factors, when present, may stop you from doing something that ordinarily you might be quite motivated to do.

Sleep, Food and Warmth

All of us get tired, hungry and cold. And when we get like that, what do we think about? Getting some sleep, food and warmth. Children are no different. If they are cold and tired, or sick and under the weather, they will not feel like doing anything much. In these situations the most powerful external motivators become useless. You can set up all sorts of rewards and incentives to encourage them to do the dishes, make their beds, help with the hoovering, but if they are sick, it just won't work, they won't do it.

Examples of De-Motivators

Cold
Hunger
Thirst
Tiredness
Sickness
Fear & Anxiety
Anger & Resentment
Low Self-esteem & Fear of Failure

Being cold, hungry or sick are internal de-motivators. They discourage us from doing what we might otherwise do. But the opposite is never true – being warm, full and healthy will not, of itself, motivate us to do anything. Just because a child is well fed, well rested and warm does not mean he will suddenly leap up and exclaim, 'I feel like doing Mom's housework for her today!'

What does this mean in practice? Don't fight with Stephen to get him to do his homework when he is tired and hungry – give him a snack and a chat first. Help him to feel comfortable first; then, and only then, remind him of the benefits of getting his homework done (see Chapter 4-2 on responsibility).

Self-Confidence, Fear of Failure, and Learned Helplessness

Children are born curious and are natural learners. Right from birth, and even before birth, the baby is taking in new sensations – the sounds, sights and smells around him, the feel of the blanket and mother's touch, the sense of being lifted, lowered, turned over – and he is putting these together to lay down complicated pathways in his brain that enable him to understand and interact with the world around him. First he studies mother's face, her eyes and her smile. He watches her lips and he tries to copy her; he sticks out his tongue when she sticks out hers.

Gradually, he gains strength and starts to lift his head and look around. Suddenly, there is a whole host of new sights to be seen. How rewarding! So he is motivated to explore further. Gradually, he learns to creep and crawl. Now he can really explore the place. But look at those adults – they go around on two feet, and it seems to be so much faster. Soon the little infant is clinging to the furniture as he hesitantly takes his first steps. Consider the immense effort involved in this. And consider how often the child fails – he stumbles, he falls, he bangs his head. The pain is a punishment for falling - for failing, but the exploration is a wonderful reward for walking - for succeeding. So he picks himself up and tries again, and again, and again.

This curiosity, the quest for new experiences and the desire to interact and communicate with the world, drives him on to new achievements. Imagine that one day you are thrust into a strange new world, knowing nothing. Just two years later, you have learned to talk – to hear sounds, to understand what they mean and how they relate to you, and to respond with your own sounds that can be understood by others. This amazing learning process does not stop there. Children go on being inquisitive and they go on learning, day after day. That they will learn is not in doubt. The question is only what they will learn.

Gradually, children learn about themselves. They learn what they can do, and what they cannot. They learn how they fit into the world about them, and how others respond to them. On the whole, children are eager to please. They naturally want to do things that make their parents, and others, happy. As a result, children gradually learn to define their successes and failures in terms of what pleases or displeases the adults. When the child first walks, not only is the experience in itself very rewarding, but also he experiences the joy and approval of others. 'What a clever boy! Look, John, our little boy is walking!' This acts as yet another reward, and marks the achievement as a success.

As we grow up, people's expectations of us change. When the six month old says 'ga-ga, goo-goo', we are delighted. We are not so impressed if a three-year-old says it.

For some children, their natural abilities and temperament seem to fulfil the expectations others have of them. They walk early, talk early, play well, and so on. Everything they try seems to meet with success and approval. As a result, they grow in self-confidence. They feel good about themselves, and are eager to try new things. Their expectation is that they will probably succeed, if not now, then with some practice.

But the child whose abilities do not match up to other people's expectations has a different experience. If, for whatever reason, she is clumsy, a poor reader, and socially awkward, she will probably not match up to what people think she ought to be able to do by now. She is learning (at her own pace), but the message she gets is that her learning is not good enough, that she is incompetent, useless, stupid. Before too long, she withdraws into herself, afraid to try something new, as she knows she will only fail anyway. Her fear

Dr. Noel Swanson

of failure becomes much more powerful than any hope of success and the rewards that come with it.

One example of this is the child with a reading difficulty such as dyslexia. Why would Susan want to spend time on her reading and spelling homework, when every time that she does try to read, she either gets it wrong, or is so painfully slow that she gets no enjoyment out of it? Would you do it in these circumstances? Or would you rather go and play with your computer game?

Along with this, the child often develops what is called *learned helplessness*. Whatever she might do or try to do, failure seems to follow. People look down on her, call her 'stupid' and other names, perhaps even bully her or beat her for being so 'thick'. She is powerless to change this, so she gives up, coming to the conclusion that this is her lot in life, and it will never change.

If this has been your child's past, you can see why she would not be very enthusiastic about learning a new skill or joining a new club. A long history of bad experiences powerfully counteracts the offer of even very attractive rewards.

This can be summarized by the following formula:

Performance + Expectations = Success or Failure

If your child is stuck with poor self-esteem and learned helplessness, then one or other of the first two factors in the equation needs to change. Either the child needs to suddenly improve his performance, or the expectations need to change. The trouble is that he cannot suddenly improve his performance – if he could, he would have done so long ago, and besides, he's only going to fail again, so why should he try? The other problem is that, by now, he has also developed his own expectations of himself which are just as high as those of others. He knows what he should be achieving, and he also knows that he falls far short of those ideals. No wonder he sees himself as a failure. Even if everyone else sets more realistic expectations, it will still be some time before he accepts these as his own. Until then, you might say, 'Well done', but he thinks to himself, 'I failed again'.

Probably the better route is to change the subject entirely. Perhaps Susan is a hopeless reader, but is a good swimmer, or good tree climber. Instead of lowering the targets for reading, why not spend more time on the swimming or tree climbing? But be careful that you do not set unrealistic goals for this too. Let her explore for herself. Let her rediscover the joy of learning at her own pace. Agree with her own self-assessment. When she is proud of what she achieved, be proud with her. When she feels she got it wrong, say, 'Oh, well, at least you had a go.' As she rediscovers her own abilities, her self-confidence will grow, and she will be less afraid to try something new and may even have another go at the reading.

Fear and Anxiety

For all humans, the highest priority is to stay alive. Some situations pose, or seem to pose, a threat to this and are therefore seen as dangerous. At these times we need to either fight the danger, or run away. To equip us to do this, our body goes on red alert. Adrenalin rushes through our arteries, our muscles tense up, our breathing becomes quicker, our senses more alert. Any unexpected sound makes us jump, while our eyes dart around to see where the danger is. At times like this you cannot just sit down and read a book; you are too keyed up.

Usually, after a while, the perceived danger passes, the adrenalin gradually washes out, and we return to a state of calmness. Once again we can pay attention to the normal daily activities.

This is also true for children. If a child is tense, anxious, afraid, or otherwise stressed, for whatever reason, his priorities will change. If Julie is worried about her dog being sick, or anxious about her SATS, or upset because her friend is being mean, she will not be her usual self when it comes to making her bed or getting her homework done. The normal motivators may suddenly seem meaningless. This is not the time to set up a new list of household chores for her to do.

This does not mean that she can get away with wrong behaviors. It does mean that in analyzing why the behaviors are happening, you will have to consider the influence of the current stress. Consequences still need to happen. Behavior is still behavior, but understanding and empathy will help her to know that you are on her side. It will be important to know that you acknowledge her feelings, that you understand that she is worried or upset, and that you are always ready to be a listening ear and a friend. It is acceptable to have feelings, but it is not acceptable to behave badly as a result. This will then help her to learn that the consequences that do happen (especially the unpleasant ones) occur not because you are mean and hate her, but because that is how life is: behaviors have consequences.

Chronic Stress

For some families, and for some children in particular, the stress does not pass. A child that grows up with abuse or violence, or who lives in a home filled with stress and anxiety, will be constantly on red alert. Life becomes about survival, not about joy and love. Learning still takes place, but in these cases it is learning how to survive.

Obviously, for these children, their behaviors will reflect their stress. Every situation is viewed through a grid of survival. They may be jittery and hyperactive, or subdued and depressed. What is certain is that they will not interpret and respond to the normal motivators in the same way as an unstressed child.

If your child is currently living like this, you need to do something about it NOW. It is meaningless to try to work on improving behaviors if the adults cannot provide a safe and secure home.

Dr. Noel Swanson

If your child has a past history of major stress or abuse, you will need to remember that it will take time for the child to view the world in a new way. Remember, when you are working out what the motivators are, do so always from the *child's* perspective.

Security and Being Noticed

Children like to be noticed. Human contact and interaction are essentials for normal growth. This makes 'being noticed' a very powerful reward. How often have you described a child's behavior as being 'attention-seeking'? That is probably exactly what it is!

When all is going well, the growing child gets plenty of love and attention from her parents. This makes her feel safe and secure, and gives the confidence to explore the world and experiment with new behaviors. Have you ever watched small children playing in a 'mothers and toddlers' group? At first, all the children stay close to their mothers. After a time, they start to get a bit braver. They go a little way out from Mom to try out a new toy or play with another child. Every now and then, however, they come back to Mom, just to make sure that she is still there. Often it's just a quick hello and goodbye and then they are off again. Later on, they do not even need to physically come back; just a quick look to make sure that Mom is there, and that she is watching, is enough. As this routine is practiced month after month, the young child gains the confidence that Mom won't abandon her, and so feels loved, wanted and secure.

On the other hand, if the bonding between mother and child was disrupted during infancy, the child will have an anxious attachment. Instead of confidently going off to play, he will cling on to mother, fearful that she might abandon him. Often mother is irritated by this and tries to push him away. This only confirms his fears of rejection, and makes him cling on even more tightly. Over time, in severe cases, this cycle of clinging and being pushed away can so seriously undermine the child's sense of security that his whole life becomes a desperate attempt to feel loved and wanted. In such cases all the external motivators can pale into insignificance in comparison to this internal need. Even so, the principles of this manual will still apply, although their success in changing such deep-rooted fears may be limited and additional professional help may be required.

The same thing happens at later ages. If all is going well at home, all the members of the family will enjoy spending time together. The children will feel that they are loved and wanted by their parents, who will play games, read stories, and generally 'mess about' with them. The result is that everyone feels secure, and this then gives the children the confidence to grow and mature.

When things go badly, the reverse happens. The fun times stop. The parents do not seem to be interested in the children, stories are not read, games are not played, Mom is too busy cooking, and Dad is out or working on his car. The children feel lost and alone. So what do they do? Kick up a fuss, start a fight, whine and complain - anything, in fact, that will get those parents to pay attention to them. It might be that they get shouted at, or even hit, but at least it shows that Mom and Dad are still around and are paying them some attention.

As you can see, this desperate need for attention can easily override the puny external motivators that you set up. Indeed, the punishments may even turn into rewards – the spanking rewards the child with your full attention for several minutes!

Anger and Resentment

If a child is angry, he will be in a state of tension, on red alert, like a child in danger. All normal priorities are therefore suspended. If a child is angry or resentful towards a parent, he may refuse to do something, even though there is a powerful external reward attached to it. Although it may seem that he is cutting off his nose to spite his face, from his perspective any consequence that results in the parent being happy is seen not as a reward, but rather as a punishment – something to be avoided at all costs, even if it means missing out on some other rewards.

Once things have got to this stage, you are in big trouble. It will take some consistent, and persistent, hard work to turn things around. But it can be done.

The Emotional Bank Account

In some ways, we are all like the high-street banks. Whereas banks open up accounts for people to put money into, we open up emotional accounts for people to put emotions into. It works like this.

Suppose you are introduced to your friend's cousin, Tom. When you meet him, you automatically open up an account for him. Perhaps Tom is kind to you, perhaps he does you a favor, pays you a compliment, or makes you feel good in some way. If he does, he has made a deposit into his account with you. Next time you meet him, you check his bank balance and find that he is in credit. So you feel happy to see him, and perhaps even feel inclined to help him or make him feel good. If you do, you will have made a deposit into your account with him, and then he will feel warm towards you. If this continues, a happy friendship will develop.

But suppose that next time you meet him, he asks you for a favor, or takes you for granted, or is rude about you. Then he will have made a withdrawal from his account. Since he is in credit, you still have warm feelings towards him. So on this occasion you are happy to oblige with the favor, or you let the insult pass.

It may be that Tom keeps on asking for favors, or keeps on ignoring you, or abusing you, or insulting you. Each occasion is another withdrawal, and so if it happens too often, he will soon be overdrawn. At this point you have run out of warm feelings. Instead, you try to avoid him when you see him, and certainly you won't do him any favors.

The same process happens at home. Every time that you spend fun time together with your child, showing him you care, you are making a deposit into your account with him. Every time you boss him about, shout at him, or put him down, you are making a withdrawal. Hopefully, you are still in credit with him. If you are, then he will love, trust and respect you. He will also be happy to help out and do you favors.

Dr. Noel Swanson

Of course the same process happens in reverse. When the children are being polite, helpful and kind, you feel warmly towards them and their bank balance goes up. When they are cheeky, rude, or disobedient, their balance goes down. Hopefully your children are still in credit with you.

Unfortunately, in some families everyone's emotional bank accounts have become so overdrawn that there is not a good feeling to be found in the place. When that happens, this is the sort of conversation that takes place:

'Tim, get down here and do the dishes.'

'Why should I? What have you ever done for me?'

'Why, you ungrateful sod! Who do you think I've been slaving away in the kitchen for?'

'So? That's your job.'

And so it goes on. With each encounter, another withdrawal is made. Sometimes the withdrawals are more like a bank robbery than an ordinary debit.

Paying off the Mortgage

When life at home has got to this stage, there are two important points to note:

1. As long as you are overdrawn on your emotional bank account with your child, he is not suddenly going to become pleasant and helpful towards you.

2. As long as you are feeling negative towards him (i.e. his account with you is in the red), you are not going to be pleasant to him. And for as long as you are not pleasant to him, you will continue to be overdrawn, and he will continue to be unhelpful.

No wonder things never seem to improve in families like this!

So what is the answer? Somehow you have to pay off your overdraft, and you have to be the one to start because you are the parent and adult. The only way you can do that is to start being pleasant and kind to your child. But you don't feel like doing that, do you? Not when he is being such an unreasonable and obnoxious brat. Quite.

So, somehow, you will need to cancel his debt to you. That's right: somehow, you will have to clear the slate, put all the swearing, abuse, disrespect, disobedience, everything, behind you and start again with a clean slate. If you don't make the first move, who will? No one says this is easy. But unless you start to find something pleasant, friendly, or complimentary to say to him, you will never start to rebuild the relationship. This does not, by any means, mean giving in to him and pandering to his every desire. You become pleasant, friendly, but you are still the parent; you don't become his slave!

The trouble is that once you have got to this stage, it is rather like having a huge mortgage – after a year of large regular payments, you seem to have hardly made a dent in the total amount owed.

So it is with people. Your first few efforts at being kind will be met with suspicion: 'What are you after?' After days, weeks, or even months, things may not have changed much. Since your child continues to be rude to you, you may be tempted to give up being nice. Don't. You will be back where you started. Little by little, if you continue to look for the good, and focus on what he does right instead of what he does wrong, and if you follow the other tactics as described in the manual, you will gradually build up your credit with him again. After a while, you might even start having fun together again!

People Still Do What They Want To Do

This section may have seemed rather complicated. Perhaps you are starting to feel that you need a degree in psychology to figure it all out.

Nothing could be further from the truth. The bottom line is still the same: what your kids are doing, they do because it works for them.

external motivators + internal modifiers ➡ behavior
(Rewards, Punishments)   (Temperament, mood, confidence,
                                    development phases)

Here are a couple of examples of this equation in action:

Katie earns 20¢ extra pocket money if she tidies her room *(reward)*. If she does not tidy her room, then she misses out *(punishment)*. She is generally an untidy child *(temperament)*, but today is feeling happy and cooperative *(mood)*, and knows that she could tidy her room if she wanted to, as she has done so many times before *(confidence)*. So today the room gets tidied.

John, on the other hand is also asked to tidy his room. If he does it, his mother will most likely say, "about &*(&)& time too!" *(no reward, in fact it is more like a punishment)*. If he does not tidy, he gets shouted at *(perhaps a punishment, but it is kind of fun to wind Mom up!)* He is generally a tidy child *(temperament)*, but today is feeling ignored and irritable *(mood)*. He has tidied in the past, when the mess has just got too much for him to bear, so he knows he can do it *(confidence)*, but today it is not going to happen.

Changing the internal factors is not easy. Some of them (like temperament) can never be changed, others, like self-confidence and resentment take time. A few, like hunger and thirst can be easily seen to.

Dr. Noel Swanson

But changing the external environment is much easier. This *is* in your control. You can choose what to reward, what to punish, what to ignore. You can choose how you will behave; whether you will command or ask, shout or talk, criticize or compliment. And whatever you do, your children will respond to.

In the next chapter we move on to the nuts and bolts practicalities of how to get started in making a happier, more cheerful home.

CHAPTER 1 - 3

Power Struggles and Manipulation

"Darren, put on your coat before you go out", instructs Mom.

"I don't need a coat", Darren replies.

"Yes you do, it's cold out." Mom says.

"So?" he retorts.

"So. You'll catch a cold. Now get your coat on. Quickly, it's late."

"I'm not putting a coat on. I don't need it."

And on it goes. We have all been there. This scene can be played out in countless variations; maybe about doing the dishes, about taking the dog for a walk, about finishing homework, or putting the toys away. Mostly it is about things that we want children to do, i.e, good behaviors that they need to **start**. But it can just as easily be about bad behaviors that we want them to stop. This might be things the child is doing right now, such as drawing on the wall or bouncing on the sofa.

Or it might be behaviors that they are just about to do, such as going out when you have told them to stay in.

The pattern is the same in each case: the parent wants something, the child does not. It is a straight conflict. Who will win? Who is the more powerful? Typically it ends in a big argument. In the end, either one or the other wins. But really, in this kind of struggle, no-one wins, as everyone has a bad feeling by the end of it.

So how does it happen? If you have read the last couple of sections you may have already worked it out: Mom wants the result more than Darren does. This means it is actually Mom's problem, not the child's. Yet Mom is trying to force Darren to solve Mom's problem. It just does not work that way.

If that were all, it would be bad enough. But there is more to this. Since it matters more to Mom than to Darren, it actually puts Darren in a very powerful position. He now has a bargaining tool that he can use against Mom to get something that he wants:

"Alright, I'll put my coat on. But only if you give me..."

Dr. Noel Swanson

This type of exchange only has to happen a few times before little Darren discovers that he can wind Mom around his little finger. Soon there will be all sorts of manipulation going on as Darren reluctantly agrees to do his homework, clean his shoes, tidy his room - but only if he gets a suitable reward. Mom, who knows how important it is for him to do all these things - for his own good, of course - sees no other way to get him to do them.

In the first chapter we discovered that people do what works for them, what provides them with the best outcome. Let's have a look at what is happening in this situation:

Darren's Perspective		
Outcome	Gain	Pain
Puts his coat on	Gets his treat (what he asked for) Wins against Mom Keeps warm	Looks un-cool
Does not put his coat on	Looks cool Wins against Mom	Gets cold (maybe)

Darren is in a win-win situation: whatever the outcome, the rewards outweigh the punishments. This being the case he can state his demands to Mom, and walk away. Whichever way Mom responds is fine by Darren.

The situation for Mom is very different:

Mom's Perspective		
Outcome	Gain	Pain
Darren puts his coat on	Happy that Darren will be warm	Has to give in to Darren's demands
Darren does not put his coat on		Unhappy that Darren might get cold Darren wins the power struggle

As you can see, Mom actually loses both ways. But of the two, the 'coat off' is even worse than the 'coat on', so she gives in and gives Darren what he wants, "Just so long as you get your coat on!"

Something has to change here! The key to this is that the **outcome needs to be more important to Darren than to Mom**. Mom needs to be able to walk away from the conflict, like Darren did, and *genuinely not care about the outcome*. Once she does that, Darren has no more leverage over her. This is how it goes:

"Darren, I suggest you put your coat on before you go out."

"No, I don't want to. No one else will be wearing a coat."

"Just a suggestion. It is cold out there, you know. But if you really don't want to, that's okay. It's your choice." All of this is, of course, said in a calm and pleasant voice.

Now the balance of power looks quite different:

Darren's Perspective - Version Two		
Outcome	Gain	Pain
Puts his coat on	Keeps warm	Looks un-cool
Does not put his coat on	Looks cool	Gets cold (maybe)

Darren may or may not decide to put his coat on. But there is no fight, no screaming or arguing. Mom simply recommends that a coat will keep him warm.

Mom's Perspective - Version Two		
Outcome	Gain	Pain
Darren puts his coat on	neutral	neutral
Darren does not put his coat on	neutral	neutral

If Darren does not take Mom's advice, it is still not an issue. If it is very cold, Darren will learn from the experience, and will put it on, of his own accord, next time. If it is not so cold, he did not need it in the first place.

The coat is perhaps a trivial (but very common) example. But exactly the same principles apply to all the other power struggles. In each case, the **root problem** is that the **outcome matters more to the parent than to the child**.

In the following chapters we will look at how to set up the environment so as to motivate your children to do the things you would like them to do. In setting it up, you will be presenting your kids with a choice of outcomes, and their associated rewards and punishments. **Crucial to this is that you do not care which choice they make.** This may be hard to do, but you will have to learn how to do it. If you don't, you're sunk. Sorry!

Dr. Noel Swanson

CHAPTER 2

PUTTING YOURSELF BACK IN CHARGE

CHAPTER 2 - 1

The New Improved YOU

So much for all the theory. Now it is time to make some changes. What is clear is that the way things are set up now does not work. So something has to change. But since you cannot change your child, all that you can do is change yourself. By changing the way that you set up your home, the rules, the consequences, your reactions and responses, you will produce a different environment for your children. In this new environment they will then have to choose new behaviors. If you have managed to set things up right, these new behaviors will be the ones you were hoping for.

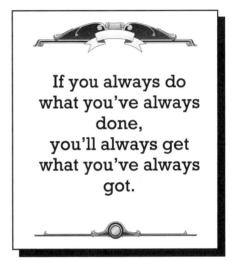

If you always do what you've always done,
you'll always get what you've always got.

So what do you do? There are two things that you aim to do in changing any behavior:

1. Break the cycle of rewards that reinforces the wrong behavior.

2. Introduce a new opportunity of rewards that reinforce the right behavior.

If you can get these two factors right, then behaviors will change. So let's start at the beginning.

BEWARE the RTP
The Repeating, Threatening Parent

The chances are that you talk too much. Actions speak louder than words, and this is never so true as when it comes to trying to motivate children. Let's go back to the situation with Johnny, who still has not started his homework.

Dad comes down the stairs and gives Johnny an instruction. The big question is, does he mean what he says? In actual fact, he doesn't. Dad is hoping that Johnny will see the error of his ways and will, out of the goodness of his heart, shape up,

Dr. Noel Swanson

get his feet off the sofa, clean up the crumbs, put his coat away, and start on his math problems, all with just a passing comment from Dad as he rushes past with the groceries.

Johnny, however, is a bit smarter than that. He has learnt, having been through this scene a few times before, that Dad does not really mean what he says, and that in fact he can probably get away with at least fifteen minutes more TV before he really has to do something. What he has learnt is that Dad is **all talk and no action!**

What happens next is the typical RTP pattern – the Repeating, Threatening Parent. Dad comes back, finds Johnny has done nothing, and so he repeats himself, only this time with a little more volume, or a little more urgency or menace. Johnny has learnt that at this point Dad still does not mean business, and so he continues to disobey.

As this fiasco continues, Dad gets more and more frustrated. His voice gets louder and louder, and pretty soon the threats get thrown in as well. 'If you don't get off your rear end right now, you are going to miss your soccer match on Saturday!'

But this is still all talk and no action. Johnny has been down this road before, and he knows that by Saturday Dad will have forgotten all about it. Besides, Dad does not want to miss the game either. So Johnny answers back, 'All right, all right, in a minute! Just stop bugging me, will you?' and carries on with his chips and TV.

By this time, Dad is about to blow a gasket. So he marches into the living room, grabs Johnny by the arm and pulls him off the couch. This is the signal that Johnny has been waiting for. Dad finally means business. But by this time both of them are pretty angry; Dad with frustration at the non-compliance, Johnny at the constant badgering and shouting. Often this can escalate into a major scene, with shouting, swearing, tears and door slamming.

The problem is that every time Dad repeats an instruction, he is teaching Johnny that he can in fact ignore the previous instruction. If you remind someone ten times to pick something up, you are teaching them that they really did not have to listen to you the first nine times as you will repeat what you said anyway! No wonder they seem to be deaf half the time – they have simply learned to tune you out until such a time as your volume or your expression indicates to them that finally, this time, you actually mean what you say.

So this leads us to some vital principles:

1)   Say what you mean, and mean what you say.

If you give an instruction, you must be prepared to follow it up with action. If you are not prepared to follow it up with action, then clearly it is not that important. In that case, either do not give the instruction at all, or put it to them as a request which clearly indicates that they have the option of complying or not.

'Johnny, please turn off the TV now and go do your homework' – this is an instruction that expects a response.

'Johnny, don't forget to do your homework, will you?' – this means nothing. Johnny hasn't forgotten his homework; he has simply decided that the TV is more fun.

'Johnny, if you want help with your math, then you need to come now' – this gives Johnny an option. He can come now and get help, or he can watch TV. But probably you will need to follow this up with a more direct instruction later on if he does not do his homework once the program finishes.

2)   Talk with a firm but quiet voice.

Take a tip from the shepherds who train sheep dogs for competitions. Have you noticed how quietly they talk to their dogs: a short whistle, a brief command? And have you noticed how attentive the dogs are to their masters' every move? Because the shepherd speaks quietly, the dog must pay attention in order to hear the command and therefore subsequently gain the reward. If you shout at the dogs, they learn that they do not need to pay close attention since you will shout loud enough that they will hear you anyway. The same applies to children. Train them to listen to you by keeping your voice down!

3)   Expect First Time Obedience.

This goes along with the first principle. If you give an instruction, you expect them to comply – now, not later, otherwise you would not have given the instruction.

4)   Follow up with ACTION.

You have given the command. You meant what you said, and you said what you meant. You have expected first-time obedience. But nothing has happened. What you do NOT do is repeat yourself or make threats. Nor do you shrug your shoulders and give up, muttering something about how disobedient children are these days. What is needed here is some action. Just what type of action we will talk about shortly, but at this point I want to stress the principles. They are absolutely crucial. Failure to follow these principles is the major reason for problems with disobedience and non-compliance among five to twelve year olds.

If you are consistent in this, the children will learn to pay attention to what you are saying, since it means that pretty soon something good or bad is about to happen, and therefore it is in their interests to pay attention to you, and they will do so – even if you speak quietly and do not shout.

Harsh, Strict or Firm?

Unfortunately, as the non-compliance continues, the frustrated parents or other adults may come out with some of these 'solutions' to the problem:

'I'll teach him a lesson, the little sod!'

'What he needs is a good kick in the pants, that's what he needs.'

Dr. Noel Swanson

'Right, that's it. Go to your room. If I see you again today, you'll get a right hiding!'

Or sometimes, the responses are less verbal and more physical: punches, belts, threatening gestures.

Of course, none of these are effective over the long term. All they produce is fear, hatred and resentment. The atmosphere gets worse, and so does the disrespect, non-compliance and defiance.

Such is the effect of harsh punishments, punishments that are excessive in respect to the 'crime' and that have more to do with the adult's anger and loss of control than with the child's misdemeanor. My friends, do not be harsh with your children. It does not work. Take some time out for yourself, so that you can calm down, before you deal with the children. If you find yourself becoming so angry that you lose control and take it out on your children, please, for your sake and theirs, seek some counseling or other professional help before you do some serious harm.

Being strict is a different matter. Strictness has to do with how many rules you have. Some people have dozens of rules about everything – do this, don't do that, don't touch this, put this away, and so on. Others are much more laid-back and have very few rules. Within reason, the number of rules does not really matter. But you will have to decide which rules are important to you and which are not.

On reflection, you may decide that many of the issues that you have been fighting over are really quite trivial. In these instances you have to decide whether the issue is really that important, or whether it has turned into a power struggle that you feel you simply must win. Does it really matter if Matthew wears odd socks to school? Is it worth fighting over every day? Or are there more important issues to deal with? Hopefully you can come to agreement on this with your partner, as what really matters is not the number of rules, but do the rules count?

This is what being firm is all about. It goes back to meaning what you say and saying what you mean. If you are not prepared to enforce a rule, then don't have it. It can't be that important if you are not willing to back it up with action.

Think about no-parking areas. In some towns there seem to be no traffic wardens at all. In these areas you know that if you park in the wrong place, or if you do not put money in the meter, there is quite a good chance that you will get away with it. In such cases people often decide that over the long haul the very occasional parking ticket works out cheaper than feeding the meter. Although there is a rule about no parking, the rule is not enforced, and so people ignore it.

In other towns it is quite the opposite. Park in the wrong place for more than ten minutes and you come back to find a wheel clamp attached to your car! Very quickly you learn that this place means business, and that when they say no parking they mean no parking. This is how your rules at home need to be. So if you do not want to be that firm about a certain rule, then scrap the rule and save yourself and everyone else a lot of confusion and frustration.

HARSH - Fear and Resentment

STRICT - How many rules?

FIRM - Do the rules count?

The Carrot and The Stick

Clearly, action is important. But what kind of action? The two main options are reward (the carrot) or punishment (the stick). But which works better? Incidentally, please understand that I do not mean that you should literally use a stick; I am using the term as a symbol to represent any type of punishment defined above.

Quick to start,
Does not last

The two actions work quite differently. The stick is the one most people tend to opt for first. The reason is quite simply that it tends to be more effective in the short term. If you want someone to dig a hole in the ground, and you stand over them with a big cudgel threatening to beat their brains out if they refuse, then the chances are that they will probably do it. However, if you were to repeat this process day after day, what you would find is that gradually resentment and anger would build up, and after a while the person might either run away or even stand up to you, despite the stick: 'Go on, hit me then, but I'm not digging this ****** hole another minute!' Punishments are effective in getting a quick response, but they tend to lose their effectiveness with time. This is particularly true when the underlying motivation for using the punishment is to **control** by inducing **fear**. With time, people become less fearful of a familiar situation and more resentful of someone trying to control them.

Nevertheless, punishments certainly have their place, and are particularly useful when trying to teach *obedience*. This will be discussed in more detail later.

Rewards are quite different. If you offer your son Tim a reward for doing a certain chore then he has an option: he can do the chore and benefit, or he can refuse but miss out. In this case he does not feel controlled, nor is there any element of fear. Instead he feels that he is in control of his own life, and feels respected and valued. The basis is therefore one of **love** and **freedom**. (Note that this is different from a bribe, which is offered to try to control and manipulate.) The only difficulty is that Tim is so delighted he has a free choice and is no longer being forced to do the chores, for the first few days he chooses **not** to do them!

Why is this? First of all, young Tim realized that to get the reward does actually require some **work**. And that, as we all know, is a four-letter word. Also, he may have been used to getting that same reward without having had to work for it. In that case, he may be

Dr. Noel Swanson

hoping (gambling) that if he does not do the work then you may give in and still give him the reward anyway.

So for the first few days you and he will have to sit it out and wait. Did you really mean what you said? Or will you give in? Does Tim really want the reward, or can he manage without it? After a while, however, Tim may come to realize that the only way he is going to get his reward is to do the work. Oh, well, such is life. And so, without any nagging by you, he suddenly gets up and announces that he will do the chore after all.

Using rewards to motivate behavior often takes a little longer than using punishments. However, the long-term effects are much more enduring. Indeed, whereas punishments tend to lose their effectiveness, rewards become more effective as the person learns to make the association between him doing things and getting a benefit as a result. Rewards are therefore used for teaching *responsibility*.

Take 'going to work' as an example. How often does your boss phone you in the morning to remind you to get out of bed in time so that you will not be late for work? He doesn't? Then how come, every morning, you get out of bed and travel to work, all on your own initiative? The reason is quite simple: you do it because you want to, and you want to because you have discovered that if you do, then at the end of the week you get paid, and if you do not, then you miss out. Now, you might grumble about it, and you might not particularly enjoy your job, but in the end you still know that it is your choice to go to work, as it offers a better lifestyle than not going. The day you decide otherwise is the day you quit.

Reward Mode vs. Punishment Mode

Remember what we learned in Chapter 1 about self-confidence, learned helplessness and the emotional bank account? If a child is surrounded by criticism and failure, he gives up. The result is a downward spiral of defiance and resentment, and a very unhappy home. On the other hand, if he is complimented and praised for his successes, his spirits soar, his face lights up, and your life as a parent is much easier.

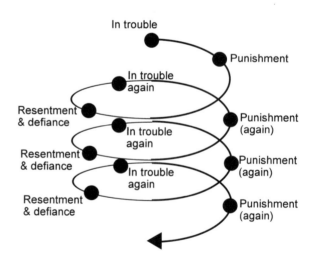

The Punishment-Mode Spiral

The lesson from this is that we need more rewards than punishments. But remember that actions are only seen as rewards if your children feel they are important. Just because you think they are rewards does not mean that they will! The goal is to start having fun together as a family. You can't do that while your children are being punished. If they are spending most of their time in one punishment or another, there won't be much time left for having fun. Not only that, but their increasing frustration and resentment will make sure that you do not have any fun when they come out of punishment either.

The only way around this is to get back into reward mode. Punishments need to be immediate and brief. The idea is to do them now, not later so that a cloud hangs over everyone. Get them over with so that you can all get back to reward mode. Do not linger over their mistakes and faults. Do not hover around, waiting to catch them being bad so that you can pounce on them. Instead, look for the positives. Try to catch them being good. Pay them some compliments. Praise their achievements.

I know, they are such horrible little brats that there is nothing good to say about them, right? Wrong. Even the most obnoxious kids have something good about them. Your job is to find it. And when you do, don't spoil it by adding an insult, for instance: 'Your hair looks really nice today – why can't you do that every day?'

Since you are out of practice, here are some sample compliments you can use. Try them. Invent your own. See how many you can say in a day.

'Thanks for putting your dishes in the sink.'

'You were quick at getting your bed made today.'

'What a nice smile!'

'How did you work that out so quickly? I couldn't have done it!'

'You did a good job on your homework today. Well done.'

'I think Timmy really enjoyed you helping him with his Lego, Paul.'

Try this for a few days and see what happens. You will find it gets easier with practice. Your target is **four compliments to every criticism**.

Who Owns The Success?

Have a look at these:

'Well done, Tim! My method really works, doesn't it!'

'Good marks on that test, Sally. Aren't you glad I made you sit down to revise?'

'Nice one! I told you that you could do it if you just listened to me.'

'That shirt I bought you really looks nice on you.'

Did you spot the deliberate errors? They might look like praise, but in fact the parent is claiming the success. It was Mom's good teaching, Dad's insistence on revision, Mom's eye for fashion that brought the success. The message the child gets is: 'You're useless, you can't do anything for yourself. You need me to sort you out.'

Dr. Noel Swanson

Too much of that and the child's self-esteem is back down the toilet. Take care, when you give rewards, praise and compliments, that you are being genuine. It is far too easy to give all of these things in such a manner that it is obvious you do not mean what you say. The words may be right, but the sentiment is quite the opposite. Obviously if you don't seem to mean it, the benefits will be lost and you will still be stuck in punishment mode.

The Informal Checks And Balances Of Home Life

In general, children know that they are expected to be helpful and polite, and in return the parents are happy to drive them places, rent videos, and provide a host of other privileges and treats. If the children start slacking off, the parents tell them to shape up. Usually, they understand what you mean and, being motivated by the desire to please their parents, they usually do as they are told.

At times, however, this informal style does not work. This happens at some time in every family. Perhaps the child does not know exactly what you mean by 'shape up'. Perhaps there are other motivators and modifiers that are competing with the simple desire to please. If family life has been rough for a long time, there may be too much fear and resentment for the child to want to comply. Whatever the reason, once the informal level of discipline breaks down, it is time to become more structured and more formal. The more severe or entrenched the problems are, the more formal and structured the solution will need to be.

The down side is that it is hard work operating at a very structured level; also, the more formal it is, the fewer behaviors can be targeted. In other words, you can either 'shape up' many minor behaviors at a very informal level, or you can try to correct a very small number of serious behaviors using a highly structured system. However, you will want to return to the informal style as quickly as possible.

And so every family will go through phases. There will be times when structure is essential in order to deal with some particular issues, and there will be times without structure. Flexibility is the key; getting stuck in one mode or the other will not work.

CHAPTER 2 - 2

Getting Started

We are almost ready to put all of this into practice with some specific strategies. Act One is about to begin, but before it does, we need to make sure that the stage has been set, the scenery and props are in place, and that all the actors know their lines.

You will have gathered by now that an important factor in getting your house back in order is that magic ingredient: consistency.

How on earth do you achieve that? After all, you are human. To be sure, you will never be totally consistent, and fortunately perfection is not essential (although it does help!). But there are some things that you can do to improve your consistency, and what is more, following these principles will also help you to be much calmer and less frustrated. This in itself will then allow you to be even more consistent. So here they are.

Recognize the Enemy

No one wants to be fighting and arguing with his or her family. You, your partner, and even your children, would all like to have a peaceful, harmonious, and fun-filled home. But something has crept in and spoilt the fun. Instead of laughter, there is shouting; instead of joy, there is anger. Soon the parents start to see their wilful, disobedient, horrible little child as the cause of all their misery. The child, in turn, wonders why he has been given such mean and bad-tempered parents. Each begins to see the other as the Enemy. Too often, I have had parents confess that they can no longer bear the sight of their child because they are so frustrated, angry and hurt. After years of struggling, their battles with their children have escalated to such a point that no one feels anything can ever improve. Sometimes the only way out seems to be to get rid of the horrible little brat!

But he is not the enemy; he hates the present situation as much as you do. The enemy is the problem that crept in and turned one against the other, spoiling the fun and eroding the love. It is true that when the hostility in the home becomes that intense it is very difficult to change. But it can be done. And the sooner you start, the easier it will be. It will take some work, and it will only happen if you are more committed to seeing things improve than to blaming the child and excusing yourself.

Another pitfall is to blame your partner. Often one parent tends to be more strict than the other. When things go wrong, it becomes very easy to blame the other one: 'If only she would be more firm with them, she gives in too easily.' 'If only he would be a bit more reasonable – he is so strict they can hardly breathe without him coming down on them!'

Dr. Noel Swanson   47

Quickly, the differences become exaggerated, and before long the parents are hardly talking to each other, and perhaps even end up separating.

But difference is not wrong. In fact, the two of you can complement and help each other by being different. But you have to be on the same team for that to happen – blaming each other will never work.

So please, put all the blaming aside, and let's start to work on making things better – for all of you. Turn the anger towards the problem, not the child, and soon you will be working together to recreate that warmth and hope for which you are all searching.

Think Ahead

Most of the time we get frustrated because we are not sure what to do next, and we know that what we are doing is not working. Once again, Katie is picking on her younger brother. If you have spoken to her about this once, you have done so a thousand times. Even as you find her at it you feel your blood start to boil, and you are already wondering what you are going to do about it this time. But you cannot just stand there watching her hit him and so, as you are trying to think of something to do, you start talking. Of course, Katie has already been through this routine numerous times, so even as you start telling her off, you know that she will simply ignore what you are saying (what was that about expecting first-time obedience?). So, as she is ignoring you, and since you still cannot think of anything better to do, you repeat yourself. Pretty quickly you are back into RTP mode.

But all of this could have been avoided if you knew, in advance, what action you were going to take instead of all the repeating and threatening. Then the scene would have gone like this:

Katie is fighting – again. Mother comes along and sees the fight, but this time she knows what she is going to do. So there is no need to get frustrated. Instead, she stays calm, and issues her instruction calmly and firmly – meaning what she says, saying what she means, and expecting obedience NOW. And she follows this up with the action that she had already decided upon in advance.

Clearly, what this requires is for you to think through your plans, in advance, while you are calm and in control. That means that you and your partner need to set some time aside to think about the children's behaviors and your responses.

This is not a one-off activity – it will need to be done regularly. Initially, as you are dealing with problem behaviors, you may need to do this once or twice every week. Later, as things become more controlled, the frequency will be less. But if you really want to get things under control, you must do this.

At the back of the manual you will find some sample worksheets that may help you to analyze the behaviors and formulate your own management strategies. How to do this will also be discussed in more detail in Chapter 5. But start now. Set aside a time when you and your partner can get away from the children and when you will be uninterrupted

48   *The GOOD CHILD Guide*

for a couple of hours. Get a notebook and write down what problems you want to address and what you are going to do about them. Then set a time and date for the next review meeting. It sounds rather formal, but unless you do this you will not be able to formulate a coherent plan of action, and you will find yourself unprepared for the next crisis.

Have A United Front.

The quickest way to produce bad behavior in children is for the parents to disagree in front of them about how to handle situations. This is also one of the biggest causes of stress and friction between parents. The child is misbehaving, so Dad blames Mom for being too soft and Mom blames Dad for being too hard. To try to contain the bad behavior, they then become more extreme in their own behaviors: Dad gets more and more rigid and possibly harsh; Mom undermines this by giving in to the child to make up for Dad's unreasonable expectations. Of course the roles might be reversed, but either way the end result is Mom and Dad fighting and the child figuring out that she can get whatever she wants if she just plays one off against the other in the right way.

How do you avoid this? The first step is to go back to the previous section – sit down with your partner and try to work out your joint responses to the situations. Then commit yourselves to supporting each other in actually doing what you have decided to do.

Get Some Support

OK, you have decided to take the plunge. You are stepping out of RTP mode and into compliment mode. No longer will you rise to the bait and start ranting and raving. The only problem is that just because you have changed today, it does not follow that the children have too. It may take several weeks for them to realize that the old behaviors do not work any more. It may take a lot longer for your emotional overdraft to be paid off. In the meantime, they carry on shouting and fighting.

So how will you cope? You were probably feeling fragile and discouraged before you started. You may feel even lower when the children seem to be getting worse rather than better after the first few days (that is to be expected, remember?). This is when you need to call on some support – a friend, relative, counselor, anyone that you can tell all your frustrations to, and who will then encourage you to stick at it.

Walk Your Talk

The telephone rings. No one answers it.

'Joanne, get the ******* phone, will you. If it's Mark, tell him I'm out,' Mom shouts down from the bedroom.

Joanne picks up the phone.

'Hello?' she says.

'Hello, Joanne. Is your Mom in?'

'Oh hi, Mark. No, sorry, she's out right now. Don't know when she'll be back.'

What did Mom just do? First she swears, and then she asks her daughter to lie for her. And then she complains that her children swear and lie all the time? As they say on the sitcoms, 'Puh-lease!'

From the moment they are born, children learn by imitating their parents. When they are a week old, it is sticking their tongues out. At six weeks, it is learning to smile. At three, five, seven years, it is learning to be kind and polite. Just like you are. And of course they learn to swear, shout and lie. Just like you do.

It is no good telling them to do one thing while you do the opposite. They will copy what you do, not what you say. Maybe they will even learn to say one thing and do the opposite too, just like you do. Children do not know which bits they are supposed to copy and which bits they shouldn't. They just follow their leader. It is up to you to be the best leader that you can. So next time you are telling them off for something, ask yourself, 'Do I need to do better on this too?'

Reset Your Expectations And Clear The Slate

Take a look at the diagram.

In this family, Jasmine is a delightful, placid, polite, well-behaved girl. A little angel, in fact.

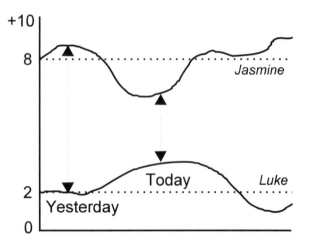

Luke, on the other hand, is a little monster. He is clumsy, noisy and hyperactive. He never does what he is told, constantly talks back, and is always getting into fights or breaking things.

On an average day, Jasmine scores about eight out of ten for good behavior, Luke only about two out of ten. Mom has tried everything she can think of, but he just won't behave. She is at her wits' end and can't cope with his naughtiness any more. She would like to have a nervous breakdown but does not have the time as she is too busy running after him. 'Why can't you settle down and play nicely like your sister?' she screams at him.

Mom's expectation is that Luke should score eight, like his sister. But he does not. Yesterday he scored two, a fairly average day for him. Since he was at two instead of eight, he was six points short of expectations. Not surprisingly, he spent most of the day in one punishment or another.

Today, Luke is actually doing better than usual. He has found a new game to play with, and instead of thumping his sister, he is playing the game with a friend. The rest of the day has still been pretty hairy, however, so he gets four out of ten for the day.

Jasmine is having a tough day. She wanted to go for a sleep-over with her best friend, but Mom said no. She is whining and complaining and generally making her displeasure felt. Today she is down to six out of ten.

On this day, Luke scores four and Jasmine scores six. Is Luke doing well or badly? Is he doing better or worse than Jasmine? It all depends on expectations. If Luke is supposed to be an eight, then he is still four points short. In fact, he is still two points short of Jasmine, even though she is miserable today. So Luke gets shouted at for all the things he has done wrong. He has failed yet again, and Mom is frustrated with him yet again. Even though he went up from a two to a four, he was punished. What do you suppose will be the effect of today on his self-esteem?

Compared to his usual average, however, Luke has done really well. He played nicely with his friend, and there were no fights. Shouldn't his achievement of getting from a two to a four be celebrated and rewarded, not punished? It is Jasmine who is far from being a little angel today – she can do much better than that!

To expect Luke to achieve an 8 is unreasonable and unfair. He has never done it in two years, so he is just being set up to fail. But he can achieve a 4 on occasions.

The Reward-Mode Spiral

Maybe if he is rewarded for today's 4 he might manage it again tomorrow. Or he might not. But if every time he reaches a 3 or a 4 he is rewarded, guess what will happen?

He will spend less time in punishment, there will be more fun times in the home, and gradually he will learn that it is more fun to behave at a 4 level than at a 2 level.

It is achievable, he has done it a few times already, and so his confidence, and his sense of self-control over his own life will improve.

This will then lay the foundations for even higher challenges at a future day. *Now* the family is in reward mode.

Where Do You Start?

What is important to you? No doubt there are a dozen, if not a hundred, large and small behaviors that drive you up the wall. Some of these will simply be irritating. Some will

Dr. Noel Swanson

be annoying, and some very worrying. On the one hand you have the wet towel that is *always* left lying on the bathroom floor. On the other hand you have playing with matches, or stealing from your purse, or lying. And then, perhaps, there is the constant complaining, whining, or swearing. Where do you start?

One thing is for sure. You cannot deal with all the problems at one time. If you try, you will likely spend your whole life in punishment and frustration mode. So obviously you are going to have to prioritize.

To do this there are three basic principles that you want to consider:

1.　**Start with something easy.** Do not dive in to try to fix the most difficult, chronic problem. Start with something smaller and then work up to the more difficult and entrenched behaviors. By doing this you can develop some confidence in your ability to change behaviors. It also means that you can quickly experience success, which means that you can then celebrate that success and so get into reward mode. If you start with the more difficult behaviors you are likely to remain frustrated with the slow progress, and then perhaps give up on the whole idea of improving things.

2.　**Decide which behaviors are the more important** over the long haul. In general these will be the behaviors that mold character and personality over time. They are also the behaviors that will impair the grown-up child's ability to function well in adult society. Lying, stealing, insolence and disrespect are obviously high on this list. Leaving socks lying around on the floor is clearly a much more minor issue.

3.　**Recognize which behaviors you can reasonably expect to change,** and which you are simply going to have to learn to live with. Remember that *you* cannot change the child's behavior. All that you can do is to change the environment around him, setting up external motivators in the hope that these external consequences will have more value to him than the internal ones that are also motivating him. In most cases that can be done. The intrinsically messy child *can* be induced to tidy up his room. But in some cases it is simply impossible.

Charles was one such child. He had a strong compulsion to dig holes in his garden. He would do this constantly and at every opportunity. All sorts of rewards and punishments had been tried in an attempt to get this behavior changed. None worked. Every day Dad would come home from work and find more holes in the garden, and every day he would get more and more angry and upset about it. In this case, the internal compulsion to dig holes was much more powerful than any other good or bad consequence.

But the behavior was causing a lot of distress to the whole family. So what could they do? Clearly, to continue to try to change this child's behavior would be fruitless. At this point some questions need to be asked:

Why is this so important? Does it harm anyone? Does it mean that the child will grow up to be a psychopath or a serial killer? Or perhaps a gardener or archaeologist? Is it just

52　　　　　　　　　　　　　　　　　　　　　　　　　*The GOOD CHILD Guide*

a phase that the child will likely grow out of? Or is this compulsion so severe that it indicates an actual disorder such as Obsessive Compulsive Disorder that may need professional help? The answers to these questions will determine the path you take in trying to find solutions.

But, whatever the answers, it is the adults who need to make the first step in changing. If it is a clinical disorder, an appointment with the doctor is in order. If it is a passing phase, then perhaps a sit and wait approach is more appropriate. Either way, it is unlikely that this behavior is going to change in the near future.

This means that if there is to be peace in the house, the parents are going to have to find a way of not becoming so upset by the behavior. The crucial first step in this is to identify that it is the digging of holes that is the enemy, and not the child. The second vital step is to recognize that the enemy (digging of holes) is causing a problem, not for the child, but **for the parents**, and in particular for Dad. From all accounts it would seem that Charles is quite happy with his hole digging - he just has a problem with his dad getting so uptight about it.

This means we can reframe the problem, not as "we need to do something about Charles digging all these holes", but instead "I [Dad] am having a problem with holes that keep appearing in my garden". Put this way, the family may be able to help Dad with his problem, instead of all of them getting upset about the failed attempts to change Charlie's behaviors.

Dr. Noel Swanson

CHAPTER 3

STOPPING BAD BEHAVIORS

CHAPTER 3 - 1

Three Counts and You're Out!

Enough of all the theory – let's get down to the nitty gritty! In this section we will discuss some specific techniques that you can use to bring a wide range of unwanted behaviors to an end. If you have skipped over the chapters on the theory of it all, you will still be able to use these techniques very effectively, *as long as you follow the instructions to the letter!* Once you have started using these techniques you should go back and read the theory chapters, as they will now make more sense to you. With that knowledge, you will now be able to further adapt and design your strategies for your own particular situation.

1-2-3-Magic!

When to Use it

Popularized in the United States by Dr Thomas Phelan, who gave it this wonderful name, this technique is used for teaching obedience: specifically for achieving immediate compliance to an instruction. It is highly effective in two situations:

1. When your child is in the process of doing something wrong. For example, jumping or climbing on the furniture, drawing on the walls, harassing the younger brother or the dog, throwing a temper tantrum. It is also useful for cutting short an argument in which the child is trying to whine, complain, and manipulate in order to get her own way – when you have said 'No' and she does not want to take no for an answer. In other words, it is used in situations where you are trying to **STOP** a certain behavior.

2. When you want immediate obedience in performing some task. These are the times when you want Susie to do something NOW, not in five or ten minutes. Be careful in using it in this situation, however, since this technique does not teach responsibility, only obedience, and most of the time it would be a bit fierce. Used too much in this situation and you may come across as a sergeant major rather than a parent. After all, often it does not really matter if the task is done now or after the TV program has finished, as long as it does get done. In those situations you can simply say, 'Please hang up your coat as soon as the program is finished', and then leave them to it. Of course, you then expect some action from them when the program does finish. If it doesn't, and they are still sitting around not doing as they were told, it is time to start the count.

For other tactics on how to start good behavior see Chapter 4.

Dr. Noel Swanson   57

What to do

1. Stay calm. Do not shout or roar. Look at the child and try to make eye contact. Give your instruction in a quiet but firm voice (the same type of voice that you use to tell your dog to 'sit'):

'Steven, get off the sofa NOW.'

'No, Amanda, you may not have a cookie until after supper.'

'The guests are going to be here in two minutes. Go and hang that coat up NOW.'

'You were told to put the game away when you were finished. Do it NOW, please.' (Just because you are being firm does not mean that you have to be rude – simple courtesies like please and thank you still go a long way to teach honor and respect.)

2. Stay where you are and continue to look at the child while you wait for a couple of seconds. Do not give the instruction and then walk away or start reading the paper. You must maintain your presence to indicate that you are serious about this.

3. If there is no action after a couple of seconds, say, 'That's one', again in a calm, measured, but firm tone.

4. Wait another two seconds while you continue to maintain your presence. Do NOT be tempted to say anything else. Especially do not make any threats: 'If you don't get a move on, you will be in big trouble. I've told you before about this so you had better get on with it' and so on. This is absolutely crucial, so I will repeat it again (I shouldn't have to as I meant it the first time, but anyway): DO NOT SAY ANYTHING ELSE. Wait in silence, otherwise you will be back in RTP mode, and you will once again be reinforcing the non-compliance with your attention. Got it?

5. If there is still no action, and the defiance, arguing, whining, temper tantrum, whatever, continues then say: 'That's two'.

6. Wait another two seconds. Do NOT say anything else. Especially do not start counting in fractions: 'That's two and half . . . that's two and three quarters ...'

7. Still no action? Then say: 'That's three – go to time-out.' At this point, especially with a younger child, you may actually have to physically pick up the screaming child and put him into time-out (see below).

8. Once they come out of time-out, the incident is over. Except in rare circumstances, you should not have a postmortem discussion on it. Instead, put the incident behind you, and try to get on with the fun stuff again.

9.   If the child goes right back to the forbidden activity, then, calmly and rationally, you simply start the process again from step one.

Notes

1.   By giving your instruction once only, and then following up with some clear action, you are able to end this incident quickly and calmly before it all blows up into a big scene. This means that both you and your child will feel better about it afterwards. Along with this, it is important to intervene early. Do not wait until the behavior is so unbearable, or has gone on so long, that you are already feeling angry and irritable. Deal with it as soon as it starts, while you are still calm, and it can all be dealt with much more quickly.

2.   Initially, you will probably have to get to 'three' on most occasions, and you may have to do this a number of times in one day. That is OK. Sending a child to time-out is not a cruel and unusual punishment. Nothing horrible is going to happen to him, and if he smartens up he can be back out again in just a few minutes and then the whole incident is over. So do not be afraid to use this as many times in one day as you have to.

3.   Children are gamblers (remember?), so for the first few days they will continue with their old behaviors – ignoring you, talking back, arguing, whining, and so on. You might do your counting and you might send them to time-out – but then again, maybe you won't follow through, and maybe this 'new phase' of discipline will wear off again in a few days and it will be back to the old-style parent – repeating, threatening, all words, but no action. So, the child gambles and waits to see what happens. Indeed, their arguing and defiance may become worse for a few days. This is to be expected; after all, these behaviors always used to work (as in getting the child what they wanted), so if they are not working so well any more, maybe what is needed is just more of them. So the volume of the shouting goes up, the swearing increases, the whining becomes more persistent.

If this happens, do not be alarmed! Do not give up after the first few days. Persist with it, staying calm, and following the instructions exactly.

After a number of days, as with the gambler, the realization comes that something is different and the old behaviors don't seem to be paying off any more. It is no longer worth the gamble.

At this stage, you will find that you get to 'three' less often:

'That's two.'

'Aw, alright then. If I have to.'

'Thank you.' (No harm in being polite!)

4.   Use this technique even if you have company. It is much less embarrassing to say to your visitors, 'Excuse me while I deal with this . . .', than it is to pretend that

Dr. Noel Swanson

Nathan is not really climbing on top of the piano with his outdoor boots on! In fact, what it shows is that although you have difficult children, you are still the boss in your home.

5.   Use this technique when away from home. Very quickly, the children will discover that once Mom starts counting she means business – at home. Ah, but does the same apply when you are out shopping? The only way you can show that you mean business when you are out shopping is to mean business – and that requires action. So, if Liam is pulling all the cans off the shelves, or Veronica is racing up and down the aisles, then you start at step one.

But what happens when you reach 'three'? Here are some suggestions.

Out Shopping:

Either,

a.   Have the child sit down in the aisle or in the shopping trolley, remaining quiet, for a few minutes while you continue shopping in that aisle. Don't leave that aisle so that she is unsupervised, but don't stand right next to her giving her your impatient attention.

Or,

b.   Abort the shopping trip. Take the child immediately out of the store, and either time-out in the car in the car park, or go straight home to do it. You will not have to do this very many times before they realize that you really do mean business! It is worth the occasional wasted trip to get these children under control again.

At a friend's house:

Either:

a.   Ask to use their bathroom as a time-out room. There is not too much damage that angry children can cause there, and they will be very surprised that you actually follow through on your word even at someone else's house! Again, it is less embarrassing to show that you are in charge, than to let the little angels run around clearly out of control. If that happens you won't be invited round again!

Or,

b.   Abort the visit and go home. This is of course especially effective if you are visiting your child's friend rather than your friend. Leaving your friend's house to go home may actually be a reward for your bored child, so if you do that, make sure that they go straight into time-out at home.

In the car:

I find that the most effective tactic is simply to pull over to the side of the road. Turn off the engine, and tell the children, quietly and calmly, that you will all continue to sit there, doing nothing, until they are behaving properly again. Then sit quietly and do NOT say any more, or else you will be back into RTP mode! Once they are compliant again, calmly start the engine and resume your journey.

6.   Sometimes children will be cheeky and will count for you: when you say 'That's one', they answer back in a sassy voice, 'That's two, that's three'. If this happens, you have two options. You can either ignore them, and continue with your normal counting routine, or you can use their count, and since they have counted to three that means they go straight to time-out. It probably does not matter which tactic you use, but you should try to consistently use one or the other. And of course you must stay calm - do not rise to the bait and get into an argument or start telling them off for being cheeky. '1-2-3 Magic' will not work like magic if you start talking in the middle of it.

7.   If after several days you are still not getting results, or if it works for a few weeks and then seems to lose effectiveness, check your technique. Almost always the reason for problems is because you have talked too much! Perhaps you have repeated yourself numerous times before you started the counting, or you issued threats and warnings, or were enticed into an argument during the counting. Any one of these is a killer for the technique.

8.   When your child has friends over, use it with them too. After all, it is your house, and your rules apply. They will learn pretty quickly what the rules are in this house, and it will demonstrate to your own children that you are not just being mean to them, but that you are fair and consistent with everyone.

9.   If Johnny is busy beating up his little sister with a frying pan, you obviously do not stand quietly by while you slowly count to three and he continues bashing her. On this kind of occasion, you skip stages one and two, jump straight to 'three', and send him off to time-out.

10.   If the school is having difficulties with your child's behavior, tell them about this system; it works just as well in class as it does in the home.

Similarly, if your child regularly goes to a babysitter or relative, try to also teach them the system. But remember, you do not have any control over what they do in their home. So if the grandparents, or your ex-spouse, refuse to use it when the children go for visits, do not panic. Just continue to use it in your own home, and let them worry about any behaviors that they get in their home. Children are not dumb, and they will figure out what rules apply in what homes and what they can or cannot get away with in each.

Time-Out

The purpose of time-out is just what it says: time out from fun and from all the rewards and motivators that were reinforcing the undesirable behavior. It is not intended to be a severe punishment that will work as a one-time cure so that this behavior never ever

Dr. Noel Swanson

happens again. For the most part, that is an unrealistic expectation for any punishment.

Instead, the goal is to break the cycle of rewards that reinforce the wrong behavior, and at the same time to introduce a reward to motivate the correct behavior. The effectiveness of using time-out comes not from one-time use, but by using it consistently – both in the sense that you do it the same way each time, and also that you do use it each and every time that you should. Remember the example of the traffic warden? If he keeps letting you off when you park illegally, then you will be tempted to continue to park illegally.

Time-out is used as a consequence for behaviors that could be classified as 'wrong', as opposed to being just 'irresponsible'. If you are trying to teach responsibility, you are much better off using logical consequences rather than time-out. Behaviors that would be classified as 'wrong' might include swearing, talking back, aggression and violence (hitting, kicking, spitting, biting), deliberate defiance (doing the exact opposite of what you have just told a child to do). Time-out is used as an integral part of the '1-2-3 Magic' strategy. But you probably would not use it as a response to Johnny not doing his homework, or Veronica leaving her dolls lying all over the kitchen floor. For these types of behavior, use the strategies for teaching responsibility.

Rules for Time-Out

1. Select a time-out room. Usually the best place is the child's bedroom, but another room such as a bathroom can also be used. It is not necessary that the room be bare and devoid of any entertainment. The goal is not for them to sit there totally bored, as if they were in solitary confinement. The idea is that they are missing out on attention and interactions with the rest of the home.

   If they come to their room and find a good book or a puzzle to get involved in, that is absolutely fine and does not detract from the time-out in any way.

   However, I would advise you to remove the TV and the computer games from the room. Quite apart from the fact that they would be too much of a reward for being sent to their room, there is in any case no good reason why pre-teens need to have such things in their bedroom.

2. Use a timer. You can use a mechanical kitchen timer, or the timer on a digital microwave. But first, you wait for the child to be quiet. Only once he has settled down and has stopped shouting and crying and banging and stomping do you start the timer. The usual rule of thumb is to set it for one minute per year of age, starting at age five. This gives the child a lot of control and thus the opportunity to develop self-control, helped along by a lot of incentive to quiet down quickly – he can either rant and rave for twenty minutes before you start timing, or he can calm down quickly and get out in just a few minutes. In this way, the reward for being quiet is built into the system.

If, after you have started the timer, the child starts up all the fuss again, then stop the timer, wait for things to calm down, and then restart the timer.

3. Once the child is in time-out, do NOT interact with her. The idea is that she has time out from getting attention from you. She may well try various tactics to engage you in a discussion or argument, even through the closed door:

'Mom, can I have a drink?'
'Dad, I need to pee.'
'Mom, is it time yet?'

Do not even be tempted to reply! Do not say a word. Do not even acknowledge that they are in the house. The only way they can get attention from you is to quiet down, wait the allotted time, and then come out. The quicker they calm down the sooner they get the attention they want.

It is permissible, however, to say the following:

'I have started the timer now. You can come out when it rings.'
'I have stopped the timer. I will restart it when you are quiet again.'

Or, after about fifteen minutes of ongoing fuss: 'I have not started timing yet. I will start when you are quiet.' (This is just meant as a reminder; use it very sparingly and very calmly.)

But again, be warned – do not get seduced into any more talking than that!

4. The child is supposed to stay in the room. If he comes out, you must calmly send him back. If at that time you had already started timing, wait for him to be calmly in his room again, and then reset the timer back to the beginning.

If this becomes a persistent problem, especially with very lively young children, then you may have to put a lock on the door in order to keep them in. The reason for doing this is that the two alternatives are to keep returning them to their room, or else to stand on the other side of the door holding on to the door knob. In both these cases you are back to giving them your full attention, and this will just reinforce this behavior!

Putting a lock on their room is not a cruel and unusual punishment. It is just good sense. Provided that you don't leave them alone in the house while you go out (which you should not be doing anyway), then there really is no valid safety concern. Don't get me wrong here – I am certainly not suggesting that you lock your child up for hours on end! If you do that, you deserve to have the social services knocking on your door. The attitude in which it is done is all important: when done in anger with a motivation of locking them away 'in jail' it is harsh and abusive. It should be done calmly and firmly, and only to give the child the message that repeatedly coming out to get your attention will not work. Once the child settles down and no longer tries to run after you, then there is no longer any reason to lock the door. To have to do this for more than two or three days would be rare indeed.

Dr. Noel Swanson

Sometimes children in time-out will wreck their rooms. Usually this means tearing the bedclothes off, emptying drawers on the floor and throwing clothes around. If this happens, do not panic. This is usually just part of the early phases of using time-out, while they are still working out if you really mean business or not. It is both an expression of their anger and a way of getting back at you for being so mean, unfair and horrible to them. Do NOT react to it; do not rant and rave at the child. If at all possible, do nothing! Leave their room exactly as it is: a mess. The issue of tidying it up again should then be put back on to them as a responsibility issue (see Chapter 4-2 on teaching responsibility). But it is best to leave the topic well alone until this particular incident is over. If you try to deal with it straight away, it is likely to flare up again into a big confrontation.

5. Getting children into time-out can sometimes be a challenge. With the little ones, you may have to pick them up and carry them. With older children, you cannot do this. In that case you may have to fall back on an alternative punishment that you are able to enforce – for example, losing all TV privileges for the day.

    Whatever the age, if there is an excessive amount of swearing, door slamming, or other abuse on the way to the room, you can calmly tell them that you have added another minute to their time.

6. Once the time-out is over, it is over. Do not inflame the situation all over again by trying to revisit it and discuss it.

Variations on Time-Out

There are a couple of variations that can be used with the time-out.
The first is for younger children. Children under five do not normally respond well to being shut up in a room for time-out. The same basic principles can still be used, but instead of a room, use a chair. Put this chair in a corner so it is a little bit out of the way of normal life, but so that they can still see what is going on. Call it the 'manners chair', as it is the place to which they can go in order to find their manners again.

When there is an incident, send the child to the 'manners chair' with instructions to come back again when he has found his manners. The child is then ignored (as with the regular time-out) until he announces that he has found his manners and wants to come back again. If he comes back without asking, then ask him if he has found his manners. If the answer is yes, then that is fine; if not, he needs to go back to the chair until he has found them.

Once the child comes back from the manners chair, it is quite appropriate for you to expect him to apologize (he may need some reminding to do this), since this would be evidence that he has indeed found his manners. If he cannot or will not apologize, then it is back to the chair to look for his manners again.

With these youngsters, try to keep it as positive and lighthearted as possible: help them to check in their pocket to see if their manners are there. Or perhaps they have dropped them, or they have fallen under the chair. By focusing on the positive aspect of finding their good behavior again, you will often be able to avoid pushing them into a corner where they feel they have to continue to be stubborn in order not to lose face. This does not mean being soft on bad behavior; it means being kind, but still firm.

The other variation is for use with slightly older children, perhaps five to nine years old. It is similar to the youngsters' version, but using the time-out room instead of the manners chair. However, you again give them the responsibility of finding good behavior. With this variation, the timer is not used. Instead, the child is sent to time-out with instructions that he may return when he can show appropriate behavior – which would normally include a spontaneous apology on his return. Until they can come up with the right behavior, they stay in their room. This variation might be used when you are trying to instil good table manners, or in response to incidents of insolence or disrespect.

You would not normally use this variation with the '1-2-3 Magic' strategy. The difference is that this variation is mostly used after an incident, whilst the counting is done while the inappropriate behavior, such as bouncing on the sofa, continues.

The 5-Minute Work Chore

This is used mainly with teenagers, or possibly with the more mature pre-teens as an alternative to time-out. First you draw up a list of work chores that take approximately five-minutes to complete. These are normally chores that have to be done, but no one likes to do them. Then, when the child is in trouble, instead of sending the child to his room for a time-out, he is assigned a work chore from the list. As soon as the chore is done, the incident is over. If he refuses or simply fails to do the chore, then he loses privileges instead.

5-minute work chores

cleaning:
  toilet
  sink
  bath
sweeping kitchen floor
vacuuming a room
bringing in the laundry
emptying all the rubbish bins
changing the sheets on a bed

Loss of Privileges

The punishments that you use must ultimately be enforceable by you. The five-minute work chore is not enforceable by you – there is no way that you can make the child clean the toilet if he absolutely refuses.

Therefore you need to have a back-up. This is where the loss of privileges comes in. All that you do is remove some or all of the child's privileges for a specific length of time. For example, you might remove their Game Boy for half an hour, or remove TV privileges for the evening. Or you may decide not to provide that car ride to their club or friend's house. Note that with the older child or teenager, this is not necessarily the same as preventing them from going; you are merely removing the privilege of a taxi service – if they want to use their own money to arrange transport then they can still go.

There are many variations on how to withdraw privileges. Do so calmly, in a matter-of-fact manner, and be firm and in control. But do not let the punishment carry over into the next day. Let each day start afresh so that they have the opportunity of succeeding and doing well, rather than starting off in punishment mode even before their sleepy feet hit the floor in the morning.

At times you may have to be quite creative in removing these privileges – taking plugs off, locking things away, hiding the keys, and so on. Just don't threaten something if you are not able to carry it through!

One final word. If your child has earned a privilege for doing one thing, you cannot then take it away again if he did something bad. If he earned it he gets it. It is the unearned privileges that you withdraw.

Avoiding Sudden Death

There is one other pitfall that you must be very careful to avoid. I call it 'Sudden Death'. This is what happens:

You have been working very hard with the children all week. They too have been trying their best, and for the most part have been polite, co-operative, and (reasonably) well behaved. As a treat and a reward for their good behavior you have all been looking forward to a special outing at the weekend.

But then Friday comes along. The morning was OK. But in the afternoon Jordan totally loses it. It starts over a petty squabble with his sister. Soon it escalates into a big fight. He hits her and she cries. You step in calmly and send him to his room. But instead of going, he swears at you and stomps off, totally ignoring you. You get frustrated, lose your cool, and, grabbing his ear, you march him off to his room amid cries, swearing and thrashing arms and legs. 'Right, that's it,' you growl, 'You are not going with us on the outing!'

So what has happened? At the last minute, all the efforts and good behavior of the week have been destroyed in one fell swoop. Instead of being able to celebrate a good week, the family is plunged into gloom over how the week was spoiled. Instead of being motivated to do even better next week, Jordan is much more likely to feel totally discouraged, since no matter how well he does, it always goes wrong in the end, and so why should he even bother trying?

Had this episode happened on Tuesday, you would probably have been able to balance it against the rest of the good week, and you would instead have been able to see it for what it is: a temporary setback amid some good progress. Overall, a time to rejoice rather than mourn. A time to say: 'Well done! You've had a good week. Only one setback this week, so maybe next week you will do even better and have none.'

So be wary of the Sudden Death Syndrome – it is more than just a day's outing that gets killed by it! To help avoid it, you may find using the points charts very helpful. See Chapter 4-2 on teaching responsibility.(page 85).

66   *The GOOD CHILD Guide*

Other Tactics

The Broken Record

This can be an effective way to stop whining and nagging, especially with younger children. This is how it goes:

Little Cathy wants a cookie. You tell her calmly that supper is in a quarter of an hour, and so there are no cookies before supper. Undeterred, Cathy asks again. Unmovable, you say: 'No cookies before supper.'

Cathy, however, is unfazed by this, and, being a true gambler, she tries again.

'Mom, I neeeeeeeed a cookie.'

At this point, you could start to count. Instead, you decide to use the broken-record technique. So you respond with the exact-same words in the exact-same tone:

'No cookies before supper.' And you carry on with your other tasks.

Cathy will undoubtedly come back many more times to see if she can win you over or wear you down. You, however, must remain a rock and continue to repeat yourself, using the exact-same words each time, just like a broken record.

As with the other strategies, the idea is that with constant and consistent use, the child will realize that you are not going to give in.

There are some drawbacks with this, however. The first is that you are still giving some limited attention to the child, since you do reply each time she asks. This attention may in itself be sufficient to encourage her to continue to ask.

The second risk is that the repetition and lack of real response from you may prove to be too frustrating for the child. In this case, it can provoke an outburst of frustration and anger which only makes the situation worse. This may then provoke you to respond instead of continuing to ignore her. If you can make it through the outburst, perhaps by dealing with it by counting, your consistency will eventually teach her that the whining does not work and is not worth the effort. She will then give up on it.

Ignoring

This is used to eliminate behaviors that are clearly attention seeking or manipulative. The three year old's temper tantrum is the classic example of this, but other examples include making silly faces and noises.

The essence of this is to totally ignore the annoying behavior. If it is a temper tantrum, you might step over the child who is rolling about on the floor and walk out of the room. If it is making faces and noises, you simply carry on with your activities. The tricky part is to genuinely ignore it. If you allow the behavior to get to you, you will start to exhibit

Dr. Noel Swanson

67

signs of annoyance, frustration or anger. The child will be quick to pick these up, and so the behavior is reinforced.

This tactic is a good one to combine with another tactic such as "1-2-3-Magic". The major behaviors are tackled with the counting and time out, the minor ones are simply ignored. Otherwise the child would feel he is constantly being picked on for every minor misdemeanor.

Grounding

Grounding (or gating, as it is sometimes called) seems to be an increasingly common punishment. Unfortunately, it is also one of the least effective. It is usually used with older children or teenagers. In its usual format, the offending child is told that he is grounded for a week (or some other period of time). This means that he is confined to home and is not allowed out to play with friends. Other privileges such as TV may or may not also be suspended during this time.

There are two major problems with this. The first is that the duration is usually much too long. The second, which is in fact related to the first, is that in practice, the full sentence is rarely carried out.

Once you have told Aaron that he is grounded, he is not going to be in a happy mood. The problem is that since you have grounded him for a week, he is going to be in punishment mode for a whole week. This provides considerable potential for him to build up his resentment and anger about the whole affair, which he will then take out on you. But since you have told him that he cannot go out for the week, that means that you are going to have to put up with his moody behavior for all that time. It is hard to build up a happy family atmosphere again while all that is going on.

The other problem is that once you have grounded him you have run out of ammunition. Supposing Aaron then pulls off another stunt – perhaps he might even climb out of the window to go and see his friends. What are you going to do then? Ground him for another week? If this carries on, pretty soon he will be grounded for life, and there is no possibility of turning this around to make it into more positive, reward-based mode.

After a few days of Aaron's griping and moaning, one of the parents will usually give in. Perhaps the grounding is just conveniently forgotten. Or some deal is struck whereby Aaron can get time off for good behavior. This last option is the best of them, but in most cases it would be better to avoid the grounding in the first place.

Instead, find something that is quick to implement and quickly over with. Now your child can experience the consequence, learn the lesson (hopefully), and then get on with good times again. And if you need to, you can use the same consequence again so you do not run out of ammunition.

There are times when grounding has its place. But use it rarely and very cautiously, and only when it is clearly appropriate for the crime.

Spanking

Now, here is a contentious issue! For some people, the very mention of the word conjures up images of child abuse. For others, it is the default punishment for any and every wrong behavior. Does spanking have a place? And if so, when and how?

In order to sort all this out, we need to be very clear with our language so that we know exactly what we are talking about. Suppose, for example, that Dad comes home from work to find Stephen once again scribbling all over the newly decorated wall with a thick black marker pen. Dad is furious. He starts shouting and swearing at little Stephen. 'I'll teach you, you little ******!' he says as he grabs him, lays him across his knee, and starts thrashing him. This is clearly not a 'spanking'. It is done in haste and in anger by a parent who is himself out of control. **Such behavior is wrong and abusive**. If you find yourself getting into this kind of situation, please get yourself some help now, before it goes even further.

So what is spanking? Spanking, done properly, is the calm, pre-planned administration of temporary physical pain without causing physical injury and without causing humiliation or embarrassment. It should not cause bruising or any other lasting injury, and the pain should be short-lived – that is, seconds or minutes, not hours. Anything beyond this is excessively harsh and abusive. It must not be done when you are angry with the child. The trouble is that in 99 per cent of cases that is exactly when it is done, and rarely does it fulfil all these criteria.

Is it effective? Not particularly. Certainly, there are more effective ways of handling behavior. With many children, it makes the situation worse rather than better; with the others, it does nothing that the other methods described in this manual cannot do better. All in all, it seems to have little to recommend it, and it carries a great risk of making things worse. My conclusion? Abandon it and work on the other strategies instead. In doing so, you will be a model of restraint and respect for your child and will develop your own self-control.

CHAPTER 3 - 2

More Serious "Crimes"

Counting and time-out work well when you catch the child in the act, or when the behavior has only just happened. But what do you do if you have just found out about something they did yesterday? And what do you do about behaviors that are clearly more serious than the run-of-the-mill fights and defiance? What happens, for example, if you find that Rory deliberately broke one of his sister's Barbie dolls to get back at her for something? Or if the children were playing cricket or baseball in the wrong place, and so the neighbor's greenhouse was smashed? Clearly seven minutes of time-out does not do justice to these situations.

These bigger misdemeanors can be divided into two groups: those that stem from a lack of responsibility, and those that reflect a lack of morals and integrity. When Rory broke the doll, he knew that his sister would be upset. That was the whole idea. He did it not because he did not think through the consequences, but because he did. He did it because he deliberately wanted to be mean. That is a *moral* issue. In our society we consider it wrong to be mean, and morals have to do with what is right and what is wrong.

Be careful to consider the child's age and maturity. Pre-schoolers have not yet developed the moral capacity to be deliberately mean. In order to be mean, you have to be able to place yourself in the other person's shoes so as to imagine how hurt they will feel when you have done what you plan to do. Pre-schoolers cannot do this. They can only think about what they want: if they want a toy, they take it; if they are angry, they hit someone. Such behavior is still wrong, and you will need to correct it so that they eventually learn the social rules of acceptable behavior. But it is only with time that they will learn to see things from another's perspective and thus develop moral reasoning.

In contrast to 'being mean', 'breaking glass' is not wrong. Often we do it deliberately, for example when replacing the old windows with double glazing. That the children smashed the greenhouse was careless; it shows that they did not think through the possible consequences of playing cricket in that spot. They must learn to be more *responsible*. What they do *after* they break the glass is a *moral* issue: do they do the right thing and own up to it, or the wrong thing, by running away and lying?

The distinction is important, as you will handle the incident in different ways. Breaking the greenhouse glass has consequences: someone is going to have to repair it. Who will pay for that? Probably an appropriate and logical consequence is that the children will have to cough up some of their pocket money for it, perhaps for a few weeks until it is paid off. They may also be banned from that location for a period of time. This type of incident is discussed more fully in Chapter 4-2 on *responsibility*. Incidentally, if the children immediately came and told you what had happened, you would also want to *reward* them for their honesty. Here is how it might go:

"Mom, Mom, quick!", they yell as they run into the house.

"What? What is it?"

"Quick. Kevin's just knocked the cricket ball into Mr. Smithers' greenhouse!", they chime.

"Oh no! Is that right Kevin?" [*It is probably safe to ask this, since Kevin has come in with the rest of them to report the accident.*]

"Yes. It was an accident, promise. What do we do? Old Smithers is going to blow a gasket!" Kevin replies.

"Well...you really should not have been playing there, it wasn't very sensible, was it? But I am very pleased that you came and told me. That was very honest, and it means that we can now try to put it right. [*praise and compliment*] Come on, we had better go around to him and apologize. Then you will have to pay for it out of your pocket money - all of you, because your were all responsible for playing there. [*logical consequence*]"

"Aw, Mom, it will take weeks!"

"Well, such is life." *(End of discussion. If they then start whining or badgering you, then you start to count.)*

Staying out late and losing things are other examples of irresponsibility. These are probably best managed with logical consequences, charting, and contracts.

Bad Morals, Disobedience and Naughtiness

But what about kids who are being deliberately mean or naughty, doing what they know is wrong? Rory is one example. Getting into fights, stealing and lying are others. Sometimes you get a combination, such as when Kevin breaks the glass, but then compounds his irresponsibility by lying and covering up.

In such cases, if there are any natural or logical consequences, they should take their course. But in addition, there needs to be some other punishment to get the message home that these types of behavior are just not acceptable.

Dr. Noel Swanson

Privileges
TV
Nintendo
Having friends round
Cubs
Swimming
Tape stories
Desserts
Pocket money
Lift to school
P.T.O.

This is where the *unearned* privileges come in. You simply remove one or more privileges, in proportion to the seriousness of the crime. Make sure that you can enforce your decision, and then stick to it. It is no use removing TV privileges if they just turn it on again as soon as you go into the kitchen.

Occasionally, the behavior is so serious that a punishment will have to last several days. This must be a rare exception, otherwise you will get stuck in punishment mode. The goal is not to find the ultimate punishment that will fix things once and for all. Instead, the idea is to give a consistent message that 'crime' does not pay (you lose your privileges) and, importantly, that behaving properly does pay, in that you get rewards and compliments, and life is much more fun. That is why it is important to get back into reward mode as soon as possible. **If you concentrate only on stopping bad behaviors and do not work on encouraging good behaviors at the same time, this whole program will not work.** You have been warned.

Note that such punishments are different to the logical consequences that follow on from irresponsibility. It is not unusual for logical consequences to last quite a while (such as paying for the broken window), because that is how life is. But such consequences need to be treated in a very matter-of-fact manner, and they do not prevent you from continuing to reward and compliment all the other good behaviors that are happening.

The difficulty with disobedience and naughtiness is that they make you, the parent, *angry*. That is understandable. But it must not cloud your judgement about the punishments. After all, you are trying to teach your children that their moods do not excuse their bad behavior, so the same rules should apply to you. If you are cross, then you should say so and express your feelings. Let them know that you are very upset and cross about what they did and why it is that you feel so cross. Not by shouting, but by talking rationally. Yes, it is difficult. But is this not what you are trying to teach them to do?

Do not let your anger lead you into a harsh punishment. This is when many parents resort to spanking, but in the vast majority of cases such spankings are not a proper punishment; they are examples of out-of-control parents venting their rage on someone who is smaller and weaker than them. Do not let it be you.

To avoid this, you may need to take some time to cool down before you decide on the appropriate punishment. It is better to do that than to be hasty by grounding them for a year.

If bad behaviors are a regular problem, you will need to be a bit more organized. To change this pattern you need not only to stop the bad behavior, but also to replace it with good behaviors. So you need a two-pronged approach. On the positive side, you will probably want to draw up a contract that details how the child can earn some rewards for the good behaviors you are trying to encourage. On the contract, you might also spell out what privileges they will lose for the specified bad behaviors.

Alternatively, you can draw up a blanket contract that spells out the punishments for minor, medium and serious misdemeanors. You could also give examples of which behaviors fit into which category. Then, when something happens, you just decide which group it falls into and dish out the punishment.

Both of these systems meet the requirements for a system that is thought out in advance, and can be applied mechanically and unemotionally, without resort to parental ranting and raving. But it does mean that you will have to set it up first. That calls for another 'think-ahead' meeting with your partner.

CHAPTER 3 - 3

Lying

There are two reasons why children lie. One is to get attention; the other is to get out of trouble. They are quite different. In the first case, children make up fantastic stories about themselves, their families and their friends. For instance, a girl might suddenly announce to her friends that her parents are getting divorced (they are not), or that her Dad has died (in a freak accident, of course). These stories get more and more elaborate with each telling, until you find out that she is actually the long-lost daughter of a famous pop star and her family kidnapped her when she was a baby, and so it goes on.

Like any other behavior, this is likely to continue for as long as it works – that is, for as long as she can impress people and get all sorts of concerned attention as a result. That is why the stories get more extreme: she constantly needs new news to tell, as old news is boring and does not demand attention.

Stopping this practice may be difficult, as you, as a parent, do not have control over the other children in her class. But you can speak to the teachers to encourage them to simply ignore it and play it down. At home, you can definitely ignore the stories, and their impact on others. Instead, you concentrate on the Start tactics outlined in Chapter 4. Reward her good behaviors with plenty of one-to-one attention so that she discovers there are better ways to be noticed than by telling whoppers. While doing this, you may also want to be thinking about the internal factors at play. When a child resorts to fantastic stories just to be noticed or get attention, it does usually suggest that there is something significantly wrong in her life – either in the present (why is she feeling so insecure and unnoticed?) or in the past (such as the anxious attachment described in Chapter 1).

The second case is more straightforward. For instance, a boy has done something and knows he is going to be in trouble. So does he own up and confess? Or does he try to hide the evidence and deny it? What do you do?

Lying usually infuriates adults. That is not good, as they usually end up in RTP mode. The funny thing is, though, that it is the adults that often set children up to lie. It goes like this:

Mother has just heard from a reliable source that Greg was throwing stones at a new girl in the neighborhood. She is not impressed.

"Greg, come here a minute, I want to talk to you!" [*Uh-oh, he's in trouble*]

"What?" he says, with attitude. [*he does not want to have this conversation*]

74   *The GOOD CHILD Guide*

"What have you been up to this afternoon?" [*What, you expect him to confess? He's not going to tell you if you don't know!*]

"What do you mean? Nothing." he says, with an innocent, puzzled, expression.

"Did you throw stones at that new girl?" [*Hmm, maybe I can get away with this.*]

"No.", he answers, startled that you could think such a thing of him.

"Well Mavis says you did."

"Well it wasn't me, it was some other kid." [*Surely she will believe her son before a neighbor!*]

"She seems pretty sure it was you."

"Well, she's wrong, it wasn't me!"

Now he is cornered. Mom has successfully tempted him to lie to wriggle out of it, and then has cornered him with the lie. It is showdown time. What will Mom do? Is she confident that Mavis is totally reliable, or is there some shadow of doubt? Greg seems to be pretty insistent, so what if it was some other kid? If she lets him off, she will have to apologize for doubting him. If she convicts him, it will have to be a double punishment: one for lying and one for throwing stones.

Most children will lie to get out of trouble. Your job is to encourage them to tell the truth, not tempt them to lie more. That means that there must be some definite benefit to be gained by telling the truth and thus incriminating themselves, rather than lying and perhaps getting away with it.

This is what I suggest. First off, you put into practice the Start tactics: get in the habit of noticing and rewarding honesty and truthfulness. As you do so talk also about the value of honesty, and a good reputation. This establishes that honesty is a Good Thing, and that it gets rewarded.

Secondly, make it clear that lying will not be tolerated, and that it will attract heavier punishments than the crime itself.

Thirdly, don't back them into a corner where they are tempted to lie. Instead, either do not ask at all, or ask in a different way.

Version 1: Don't Ask

Don't ask If they have been caught red-handed, and there is no doubt whatsoever that they did it, do not ask them, 'Did you do it?' You already know they did it, so why give them the temptation to lie and try to wriggle out of it? If you want, you can ask, 'Why did you do that?' But you probably will not get a sensible answer. Better just to get straight to the punishment. 'I saw you throw stones at that new girl. That is not on! I am very

Dr. Noel Swanson

disappointed in you. As a punishment, you can either vacuum downstairs, or you can go to your room for the rest of the evening.'

At the same time, you can acknowledge the feelings that motivated the behavior. Remember, it is OK to have feelings, but feelings need to be talked through or dealt with appropriately, not acted out with antisocial behavior. After the punishment, once things have calmed down, you might say, for example, 'You must have been pretty angry with that girl to make you want to throw stones at her.' This may then open up a very useful conversation about the feelings and frustrations that he has and has not known how to deal with.

Version 2: Ask for the Truth

Ask for the truth 'Greg, I've just had a very disturbing phone call from Mavis about something she saw this afternoon. I would like to know what happened. But before you tell me, I want you to go away and think about it for fifteen minutes. Then we can talk about it and see if we can sort out the feelings that you were having at the time. And remember, we value honesty in this household.'

Mom has made it quite clear that she knows something and is not impressed by it. But she has also made it clear that the usual rules about honesty apply; you tell the truth, you get a minor punishment for the misdeed, and you get praise for your honesty; you lie, you are in big trouble. She is also acknowledging Greg's feelings and giving him an opportunity to talk about them and to learn the right way to deal with them. By giving Greg fifteen minutes to think about it, she is not putting him on the spot, where the first reaction might be to lie.

Hopefully, during this time he will decide that honesty is the best policy. If he still decides to lie about it, then it's the high jump: 'Greg, I am disappointed in you. Why are you lying about this? As it is, I am going to have to suspend all privileges for the rest of the week.'

CHAPTER 3 - 4

Stealing

When is a thief not a thief? When he stops stealing? No, then he is just a thief taking a break (or in jail). A thief is no longer a thief when he becomes honest.

Stealing ranks right up there with lying as a sure way to get a parent's blood to boil. If it is happening in your family, it is probably at the top of your list of behaviors that you want to stop. Yet, like lying, it is better managed not by focusing on stopping it, but rather on promoting the opposite, which is honesty.

Children steal for a variety reasons. Some steal for comfort. For them, the stolen goods (often of little financial value) replace the love and affection of which they have been deprived. Others steal to impress a group of friends, or to get back at their parents, or to get the things they want, or just because it is exciting. Probably as many as one in four children have deliberately stolen something at some time. Often it is just some sweets from a shop, but they knew, as they did it, that it was wrong. Most, of course, never do it again. But those who do, do so for one reason: it works. Whatever their core need, attention or money, the stealing provides it for them.

Once again, we do have to consider the child's developmental age. As with lying and "being mean", a child of two or three cannot *steal.* He can take things that are not his, for sure, but because of the lack of moral development this is not stealing. To label it as such just inflames the situation. Similarly, a child of three or four is only gradually learning that he is not supposed to take what belongs to others, again the word *stealing* is probably unnecessary and unhelpful. It is only when the moral understanding that it is wrong develops that it can be called stealing. This understanding is most easily seen by the need to cover up the deed. The infant does not cover it up - he does not know it is wrong and so does not know he should be hiding what he did. The eight year old knows very well it is wrong, and so does it secretly.

So how do you stop it? The first problem is that you cannot catch them every time. This makes it hard to eliminate the rewards that they get out of the stealing. All that you have done is add in the gamble factor. So they get caught sometimes. But maybe the other times more than make up for that. The second difficulty is that if the stealing provides them with attention or excitement, then you making a fuss about it may actually end up in rewarding the habit! True, your attention might be rather negative but, as we learned in Part I, any attention is better than none.

As with lying, your main emphasis needs to be on promoting honesty. That means you talk about it as a family, not as a lecture, but as a discussion when the occasion presents.

Dr. Noel Swanson

77

Use everyday events such as items on the television, or stories from school as a starting point for discussing the family's morals.

At the same time, you model it yourself. What do you do when you find a wallet in the street? Or when you are given too much change in a shop? Or when a workman offers to do the job for cash, with no tax? Your children will be watching you, and learning.

Then you watch your children. Not to catch them out, but to catch them being good. Then you can reward and praise the little acts of honesty that you see. As with the lying, all of this promotes a culture of honesty in the home.

But what happens when they do get caught? The first thing is to stay calm. Losing your temper will not help, and may even act as a reward for them. Secondly, do not compound the situation by cornering them into a lie.

After that, you need to *do something*. What is an appropriate response to stealing? In the Bible there is a delightful account about Zaccheus, a corrupt tax collector. Zaccheus, who was only short, climbed a tree so as to see Jesus as he passed by through the crowds. Jesus spotted him, and invited himself to his house. Suddenly, Zaccheus was so overcome by his guilt that he resolved, not just to stop stealing, but even to pay back everyone he had cheated **four fold**. Truly, Zaccheus became an honest man that day.

Zaccheus gives us a clue here. It is the principle of **restitution**. This means putting it right. Not just paying back what was stolen, but also paying compensation for the inconvenience and disrespect caused by the theft. If at all possible, the child should do this himself, probably with your accompaniment. For example, going back to the shop, meeting the manager, confessing the crime, and giving him the stolen goods plus compensation. This will not be an enjoyable experience. If that is impossible, for example, if it was taken from a stranger, then you will simply have to confiscate the goods and fine him the extra. Make sure that you get rid of the stuff so that it is not around in the house, still to be enjoyed. Alternatively, he could take the stuff to the police station.

Taking the stolen property back is his opportunity to do the right thing. He may refuse to do this. In that case you have no alternative but to impose an even higher penalty. The message must always be that doing the honest thing, even if it is after the event, is still the best policy. Even while all this is going on, you can still be looking for opportunities to praise him for when he is getting it right.

In some instances the child has already disposed of the goods and spent the proceeds. Then maybe he will have to sell (perhaps to his parents) some of his own possessions to raise the money to put it right. If you take that route, make sure the things he sells do go permanently and do not reappear a few days later. If he wants them back, or wants replacements, he will have to earn the money and buy them.

If at all possible, try to deal with it by making restitution someway or other. If he really has no money left, and nothing to sell, then perhaps he can do some "community service" for the person he cheated (or, as a substitute, for the parents or neighbors).

If at all possible, try to avoid a long grounding sentence. Jail does not reform hardened criminals, and grounding will probably not reform your own little angel.

If stealing is a persistent problem, you will need to draw up a contract on it. You may also need to lock your doors and drawers so that you do not put temptation his way.

Finally, once it is over, get over it. Back into reward mode, and work hard at reinforcing honesty. It is the stealing that is the enemy, not your child.

CHAPTER 4

STARTING GOOD BEHAVIORS

CHAPTER 4 - 1

Seven Strategies

Just to remind you, the principles for changing behaviors are:

1.   Stop rewarding the bad behavior, and

2.   Start rewarding the good behavior.

There are seven tactics for encouraging good behaviors. Each is particularly suited to certain types of behavior, but they can also be used in various combinations. Since the good behavior is often the opposite of a bad behavior, you may also want to combine them with some of the 'Stop' tactics. For example, honesty is the opposite of lying and stealing, so you will want to reward their honesty, and also punish their dishonesty.

These are the seven:

Praise and Compliments
Make it a Game
Natural Consequences
Logical Consequences
Charts and other Contracts
Payment
1-2-3-Magic

Each of these have their place. Which do you use for which behaviors? As a general rule, it works like this:

Behavior	Motivator	See Page:
Being pleasant, friendly, helpful, generous	Praise and Compliments	102
Smallish tasks that you usually have to nag them to complete	Make it a Game	99
Being responsible for possession, homework, money, getting to school, etc.	Natural consequences Logical consequences	87 88

Dr. Noel Swanson   83

Behavior	Motivator	See Page:
Taking care of regular tasks, e.g. getting to bed on time, household chores, homework, walking the dog	Charting	90
Obedience - getting some small task (less than 2-minutes) done right now.	Make it a Game 1-2-3-Magic	99 57
Integrity, honesty	Praise and Compliments	102
Doing a larger task when asked, e.g. washing the car	Contracts Payment	96 98

In the following sections these tactics are discussed in detail. I have started with the more formal ones, as you will need to begin with these to get you out of punishment mode, and to get some good routines going in your home.

Once things are running a bit more smoothly, you will want to move on to the more informal and enjoyable ones. These will get you well established on the reward-mode upward spiral, and will help to promote longer-term good behaviors and a happy home atmosphere.

CHAPTER 4 - 2

Responsibility

"Jody, your room is a mess!"

Jody's messy room presents us with two concerns:

1.   If she does not learn to keep her room tidy, things will get lost or trodden on. She needs to learn to be responsible about her possessions. As a caring parent, you worry about this. If she does not learn to be responsible, she will have problems as she grows up. Jody may not realize this yet, but her lack of responsibility is her problem.

2.   You cannot stand the sight of the messy room. It offends your tidy nature, and is an embarrassment when visitors come around. Jody may be the one that gets shouted at, but it is you who gets irritated by the mess, not her. Your irritation is your problem.

It is important to distinguish between these two concerns. If you do not, you are likely to end up in a classic power struggle. Because you hate the mess, getting the room tidy becomes more important to you than to Jody. Before you know it, you are back to trying to get Jody to solve your problems for you. Can you give her one reason why she should?

If the mess is really so irritating to you, you have three options:

1.   You can leave the room a mess (perhaps with the door shut?).

2.   You can tidy it up yourself.

3.   You can try to persuade someone else to do it for you.

Now, we already know that we cannot make anyone do anything, and since Jody is not motivated to tidy her room herself, the only way that she will do it for you is if you pay her in some way. Since you are wanting someone else to fix your problem for you, this is really quite reasonable.

Instead of the power struggle, it would be much more honest to try it like this:

Dr. Noel Swanson

'Jody, I know you are happy with how your room is at the moment, but we do have some visitors coming round. I would be very embarrassed if they saw your room like that, so would you do me a favor and tidy it up?'

In this instance, Mom acknowledges that it is her problem, not Jody's, and that she is making a withdrawal from Jody's emotional bank account by asking her for a favor. As we have already seen, this ends up as being a much smaller withdrawal than it would be if Mom forced her to do it.

Of course, Jody will not learn anything about responsibility from this occasion. To teach that, we have to go about things a different way.

What is Responsibility?

Responsibility is about having a choice and living with the consequences. Almost always, it is about something that we do not really want to do, but the consequences of not doing it are worse than the hassle of doing it. As we saw in Chapter 1, we are constantly faced with responsibilities: providing food for the family so you don't starve; paying the taxes so you don't go to jail; getting the car serviced so it does not break down; keeping the house clean so you do not get rats and mice.

The only reason you do these things is because if you don't, no one else will. If someone else kept stepping in to bail you out, you would never learn to do it for yourself. The same is absolutely true for your children.

When your children were babies, you took full responsibility for them: it was up to you to make sure they were fed, cleaned, clothed and safe. When they turn eighteen, hopefully you will not be taking any responsibility for them – it will be up to them to make sure that they are fed, clean and safe. It will also be up to them to make sure that their belongings are safe, that their bills are paid, that they get to work on time, and all the other things that adults need to attend to.

Note this carefully: as an adult, your child **will** be responsible for her actions, or lack of them. That is to say, she will be faced with all these tasks; it will be up to her if she does them or not, and it will be down to her to live with the consequences if she doesn't. You may not like the choices she makes. You may wish that she would take better care of her things, that she would look after her money better, and so on. But, in the end, it is none of your business! That is the essence of responsibility. Your child still has the responsibilities, even if she behaves irresponsibly towards them.

When they grow up, your children will assume these responsibilities. Since that is the case, it would make sense to gradually prepare them for the fact. Also, it would be nice if they could learn to act sensibly and not foolishly with regard to them.

How do they learn to act responsibly?

Responsibility is learned by having responsibility.

There is no other way. What does this mean? It means gradually giving your children more and more responsibilities – and then stepping out of the picture. This is the time to let them sink or swim. If they fail in the task, do not step in to help them out; let them fail. It is the only way that they will learn that it really is their responsibility. Hopefully, next time they will choose to do it properly.

There is, of course, one vital proviso in this: the child must be **capable** of doing it. Responsibility is not a question of 'Can he or can't he?' but of 'He can, but will he or won't he?' Otherwise, you are setting them up for failure.

What happens if they make the wrong choice? Then there will be consequences. That is the whole point about responsibilities. That is, after all, how the world works.

Natural Consequences

If you leave your bicycle outside instead of putting it away, one of two things may happen:

1. It may get stolen. If that happens, you have no more bicycle!

2. It may get rained upon and go rusty. If that happens often enough, your bike will stop working, and guess what? No more bicycle!

Neglecting the care of your bicycle can lead to unfavorable consequences. These consequences are entirely natural. They occur not because Mom or Dad is being mean, but simply because that is how the world is. These natural consequences, being unpleasant, may act as punishments in that they may well teach you to stop that particular behavior and replace it with another one – such as looking after your bike properly.

Many of our behaviors have natural consequences: if I am rude to people, they won't like me; if I tell lies, people won't trust me; if I am kind and generous, people will be kind and generous to me. If I run out into the road, I will get hurt, have to spend weeks in bed, and so will miss out on having fun. If I look after my belongings, they will last longer, and I will save money by not having to replace them, and so on.

It is because these consequences happen that you hope your children will grow up to be sensibly responsible.

Often, it is wise to simply let your children experience the natural consequences for themselves. We talked about this when we looked at power struggles: it is much better to let the child get cold than to have a big fight about putting a coat on. With time, he will learn to avoid getting cold by putting his coat on. Or he will decide to put up with being cold in order to look cool. It then becomes his choice, his responsibility. Once he is old enough to argue about it, he is probably old enough to decide for himself. Another example is letting the infant touch the hot kettle. You could keep on telling her 'no', and

---

Dr. Noel Swanson

you could move the kettle out of the way. But at some point she has to find out for herself what happens when you touch something that is hot.

Your child will make many mistakes. On some of these you will simply want to step back and let the consequences follow. This is called 'learning by experience in the School of Hard Knocks'! Your job, as the parent, is to wisely choose which knocks the child can learn from at this time, and which ones are simply too difficult or too dangerous for now. You do not give a four-year-old a blow torch so that he can learn from the experience of burning the house down. It is not easy deciding at what age you can give children various responsibilities. However, as a general rule, if you are getting into repeated power struggles and conflict over an issue, it probably means that it is time to find a way to release them into that responsibility.

Allowing natural consequences to take their place is the first tactic for teaching responsibility. Do not be overprotective – let them go a bit, so that they can learn for themselves.

Logical Consequences

The problem is that the natural consequences may not happen all the time and are often unpredictable. The first few times you leave your bike out, it does not rain, and the thief does not pass by. Indeed, it will take many weeks of rain before the bicycle seizes up with rust.

When the natural consequences are infrequent, or delayed, it is often difficult to learn from them. The children with an easy temperament have it somewhat easier as they start off on the right footing. For example, being natural, calm and pleasant, they discover that people respond well to them, and so their good behavior is quickly rewarded.

Other children find it a bit harder. So, with them, we have to give nature a bit of a hand. What we do is to apply artificially (i.e. by our own intervention) a consequence that in some way mimics the natural consequence. In other words, it is a logical consequence. For example, the natural consequence of leaving your bike outside is that you lose the use of it. Therefore the logical consequence for leaving your bike outside is that you lose it – only this time it is because Mom and Dad have locked it up for a day or two. You can have it back on Friday, but if you leave it out again then you will lose it again. After this happens a few times, you will start to be a bit more diligent in putting it away! As you can see, this consequence is much more logical, and is therefore a more fitting and effective punishment, than, for example, losing TV privileges or being sent to bed early.

Once again, the key to this is that Mom and Dad really do not care if you have your bicycle or not. It is entirely up to you. You can decide for yourself to either put it away, or leave it in the driveway, and what is more, **Mom and Dad will not yell or nag at you!** What a relief for you all.

Logical consequences can also be rewards. In fact, using the earning of privileges as a motivator is actually using logical consequences. In general, if you scratch my back, I'll scratch yours; if you pull your weight and chip in, helping out with the chores and

88   *The GOOD CHILD Guide*

responsibilities of this place (whether home, office or social club) then you will get to benefit from it. If you sit back and let everyone else do all the work, then after a while they will stop including you in the privileges and benefits, as they will view you as someone who is 'sponging' off them. This is part of the natural balance of life, and would normally be part of the informal checks and balances of the home.

When things are not going so smoothly, then it may be time to use some artificial consequences. You will then spell out exactly what you mean by 'shaping up and helping out' and you will also spell out exactly what benefits they will enjoy as a result of pulling their weight. By doing this, you make a much clearer connection between the 'helping out' and the 'benefitting'. One way to do this is by using a system of charting.

CHAPTER 4 - 3

Charting

Charting is used to establish regular routines of good behavior. It takes a bit of time to set up, but once you have done so, it makes life **a lot** easier. The children like it too. This is for two reasons: first, it puts them back in control of their own lives, and second, Mom and Dad do much less shouting.

This is the deal: you define what jobs they should be doing. If they do them, they get a reward. If they do not, then they miss out. Once it is up on the chart, it is then up to them whether they do it or not. They have the choice, which therefore makes it their responsibility.

Your part of the deal is to be quiet. That means no shouting, 'Richard, get down here and do the dishes!' It means sitting down, reading your paper and letting them get on with it. Or not, as the case may be.

On page 141 you will find a sample template that you can use. Below, I have also put a real-life example to which you can refer. Do a separate chart for each child and, if you can, involve the children in putting it all together. Here is how:

1.   Make a list of all the daily tasks, chores and responsibilities that you want them to be doing. Now cut the list down to a maximum of eight that you want to work on at this time. Make sure that they are all well within the capabilities of each child.

2.   For each item, define exactly what you mean by it and by what time it must be done. For example, what exactly does 'tidy bedroom' mean?

3.   Give each responsibility a points value of between one and four, depending on how important it is.

4.   This is the tricky part. Decide on their basic rights. Their basic rights are what they get if they have a totally rotten, awful day. They include such things as food, water and a bed. Do they include such things as TV and computer games? That is up to you, but remember, if it is on the list of basic rights, then they get it whatever happens. Once you have decided on the rights, all the rest are privileges. Some of these you will probably give them anyway, just because you are kind and love them. The rest have to be earned.

5.   Decide what rewards and privileges they can earn based on their points. I suggest that you choose four: three that can be earned daily, and one weekly bonus (see page 137 for suggestions). Note that the daily rewards do not have to cost any

90   *The GOOD CHILD Guide*

money. In fact, it is probably better if they do not. Be careful what you choose. If they don't earn it, they don't get it. It is no use making 'go to swimming lesson' a reward unless you are genuinely prepared to not send them if they do not earn the points. Also, make sure that you are able to enforce the withdrawal of a privilege if they do not earn it.

Those that you do not use for the chart are 'unearned privileges'. It is useful to have a few of these up your sleeve for taking away if they have been exceptionally bad (see Chapter 3-2, on 'More Serious "Crimes"').

6. Set the targets. The goal here is to encourage them, not frustrate them, so do not set impossible targets. Take a close look at the points that they could earn. In the example below, Ben could earn up to fourteen. Now take a guess at how many points your children would actually earn on a typical day at present. Take today as an example. How many points would they have earned? Perhaps you figure on about eight. Whatever the number, that should become your first target. Why so low? Because you want to make it easy for them to succeed. Since you want to be in reward mode, it needs to be fairly easy for them to get the first reward. That makes them feel good, and it encourages them to try a bit harder in order to earn the higher rewards. If you make it too difficult, they will just give up and not bother.

    Having set the first target, you then set the other two. In the example shown, Ben missed the first target on the first day, so he went without. Tough day. The next two days he did a bit better and got his chocolate mousse. Then on Tuesday, there was a dramatic improvement. Well done, Ben! Now he gets all three rewards, and everyone can be feeling good and passing around lots of praise and compliments.

7. Decide on the weekly bonus. My recommendation for this is that you multiply your middle reward (in this case eleven), by seven. Essentially what you are saying is that they can earn the weekly bonus if they can maintain a B-average for the week. This helps you to reward sustained effort, and also helps to avoid the Sudden Death syndrome (page 66).

8. Decide at what time you will check the chart and award the privileges. This should be at the same time each day. Often supper time is best, as that gives them the evening in which to enjoy privileges. Any points earned after this time count towards tomorrow's total. You will see on the chart that the first few responsibilities were actually done yesterday evening and the points earned carried forward for today's rewards.

9. Explain the deal to the children, stick it up on the fridge, sit back, and see what happens.

THE DEAL   Benjamin

Responsibility	Pts	Sat	Sun	Mon	Tues	Wed	Thu	Fri	Total
<u>Last night:</u> Reading & Spelling	2		1	1	1	2	2	2	
Clear table in 10 minutes	I	1	1	1	1	1	1	1	
Go to bed without fuss	2	1	1	1	2	2	2	2	
Stay in bed without fuss	**3**		2	1	3	3	3	3	
<u>Today:</u> Get dressed in morning	2	2	1	1	2	2	2	2	
Bathroom stuff	I		1	1	1	1	1		
Ready for school by 8:15	I	1		1	1	1	1	1	
Good day in school	2	2	1	2	2	2	2	2	
Daily Totals:	14	7	8	9	13	14	14	13	78

Rewards	Pts. Needed
chocolate mousse for dessert	8
Extra 20 min story time or tape story or Game Boy	11
1/2 hour computer or TV time and 1/4 hour later bedtime	13
Fun City	77

Notes and Definitions
One point each for Reading and Spelling
One point docked for each time out of bed
Ready for school means hair and teeth done, shoes and coat on, and school bag packed.

Remember the Rules:

1.   **No nagging, shouting or arguing.** It is their choice to do the chores and earn the points, or equally to not do them and not earn the points. This is how it is. Your job is to sit back and let them make their own decisions.

2.   **If they have earned it, they get it. If they have not earned it they do not get it.** No exceptions. None.

So what happens?

First, they will whine and complain. You are asking them to do something that they do not want to do, and you are threatening them with the removal of what you see as privileges but they see as rights (like the television). They will probably try all their old tactics for getting what they want, like arguing, sulking, shouting, whining, and so on. After all, they always used to work. You, of course, will stand firm, and silent (you would not fall into the trap of trying to argue or reason with them, would you?).

They will then say, 'You mean, we don't have to do these if we don't want to?'

To which you reply, 'That's right! It is entirely up to you.'

They then scamper off, muttering, 'This is great! No more chores!'

Now comes the test for you. It is 6 o'clock. You have just finished supper. The Deal says that it is Lucy's job to clear the table, and she has half an hour in which to do it. On the first few days you can calmly remind Lucy, 'Don't forget to clear the table if you want your points'. After the first week, do not even say that. You just get up, go into the living room, and watch the news. You do not shout up the stairs, 'Lucy, get down here and clear the table!'

Lucy, meanwhile, decides that she would rather read her comics than clear the table.

At 6.30 p.m. you pop your head around the door. The dishes are still on the table. Oh, well. Lucy does not get her points, and you do the clearing up instead.

The next day, Lucy wants to watch her favorite program on TV. The trouble is that she does not have enough points.

'Sorry, Lucy, you don't have enough points for TV today.'

At this point she will probably try one of the old tactics to get you to give in. You stand firm and silent. She may well say, 'Fine, then. I don't care', and stomp off to her room. Or she may make a scene and have a temper tantrum, at which point you say: 'That's one.' Either way, she does not get the TV.

The next day it is the same story. Dishes still on the table. We now enter the waiting game. Lucy gambles that eventually you will give up this ridiculous system and give her the TV privilege without her doing the job. You are quite happy for her to go without TV, and are also happy to clear up – after all, she was not doing it before you started the chart. And it is much more peaceful not having to nag her all the time.

Eventually, having tried all the other tactics, Lucy realizes that the only way to get to watch the TV is to earn her points. Suddenly, without being asked, the table starts getting cleared. Lucy earns her TV. Praise and compliments all round.

Dr. Noel Swanson

Common Questions

What about weekends?

What about weekends? Weekends often have a different routine to weekdays, so you may want to use two charts. Or just use one chart, defining some tasks as weekend tasks and some as weekday tasks. Make sure that the totals still add up, though, so that they can still earn all the privileges whether it is a Sunday or a Tuesday.

Why isn't it working?

By this, people usually mean that the child is choosing not to do the tasks. First, make sure you are following the rules: no talking or showing emotion, and make sure they get what they earn and don't get what they don't earn. This means you will have to choose rewards that you are effectively able to enforce. It may mean taking the plug off the TV for a while.

If you are doing all this, then the system is working. It is just that the child is choosing to not work and not get paid, rather than to work and get paid. That is allowed; it is his choice. There are four reasons why this might be happening:

1. You have not been operating the Deal for long enough. You are still being tested to see if you really mean business with this new idea of yours. Give it about two weeks before you get worried.

2. The targets are too high or the tasks too difficult, so the child just gives up (see also page 50 on setting expectations). Set easier tasks, or lower the points needed for a reward.

3. You have picked the wrong rewards. The child is genuinely not interested in the treats you have offered. Either that, or they are just not good enough to be worth all the work involved, especially if the tasks are big, like cleaning their room. It is worth sitting down with the children and asking them what rewards they would like to earn. It is surprising how often they will co-operate with this, and then you have a reasonable chance of offering something that they do care about.

4. The Deal is fine. The problem is that there are other modifiers at work, undermining the incentives. This is the time to check things out more carefully: are there problems at school, like bullying? Is she worried about her SATS? Have another look at Chapter 1.

It worked at first, but now it doesn't

Most likely, you are no longer keeping your part of the bargain. Check the two basic rules again.

How long do we do keep this up for?

You do not want to be charting for the rest of your life. The idea is to establish some routine, and then to get back to the normal informal checks and balances of living together. It usually takes a couple of weeks for the charts to kick in. Ideally, you want to have it running smoothly for a few weeks, and then you will probably want to stop it. It depends how bad it was to start with and how well you are doing with all the other tactics described in this manual. Do not just drift out of it by getting slack on the rules. Either do it properly, or stop it altogether.

My suggestion is that you discuss the termination with your children. See what they think. They may want to continue with it, as they like the praise and compliments they have been getting, and they are delighted that you have stopped nagging. They will want some assurance that those aspects will continue!

Variations on Charting

The Star Chart

You have probably used this with your children when they were young. It is in principle the same as The Deal, but with the following differences.

1.   It is used with a smaller number of target behaviors – often only one, such as 'had a dry night'.

2.   It uses stars instead of points. Instead of awarding the privileges each day, the rewards are handed out whenever a certain number of stars have been reached. You start with a small number (maybe even one) and then gradually build up to needing more in order to get the rewards.

There are two ways to do it. One way is to require all the stars to be in a row – for example, three dry nights in a row. This is fine if it is only a small number, such as three or four. If it is too many – as in the diagram, where six stars in a row are needed to earn a reward – then you risk Sudden Death: they have a long string of stars, only to fail on the last one, and so get no reward at all.

Star Chart, Type 1

	M	T	W	T	F	S	S	M	T	W	T	F	S	S	M	T
Made the bed need 6 in a row	★	★		★	★	★	★	★		★	★	★	★	★	★	

Sudden death; no reward ↑   *Start again*   *Made it!*

The other way is to reward the child whether or not there are gaps in between. If you manage it without gaps, you get your rewards more frequently. If you fail sometimes, don't get discouraged; you will still get rewarded for your successes, it will just take a little longer. But at least it avoids the Sudden Death Syndrome. One variation of this is to have a picture, for example, of a clown juggling some balls. When each ball has a star in it, then you get your reward.

Star Chart, Type 2

	M	T	W	T	F	S	S	M	T	W	T	F	S	S	M	T
Made the bed need 6	★	★		★	★	★	★	★		★		★	★		★	★

reward ↑   reward ↑

Progressive Privileges

This is like a combination of the Deal and the Star Chart, type 1. The idea of this is to encourage consistency, once they are doing well, whilst still targeting a number of behaviors. The set-up is identical to the Deal. This time, when they score the first-level reward, stick a red star onto the chart (get them from a stationer's). If they earn the middle reward, give them a green star. If they earn the top reward, give them a blue star. All in addition to the rewards, of course.

Now comes the fun. If they earn, say, seven blue stars in a row, then instead of blue stars you stick on a gold star. This means that they get an even higher (fourth) level of privileges. For as long as they keep earning a blue star, *without a break*, keep giving them a gold one. But if one day they drop down below a blue, then it is back to the start. They will have to earn another seven blue stars *in a row*, before they can climb back onto the gold level.

As you can see, once they are getting gold stars, there is a good incentive not to drop back down again.

Contracts

Charting is used for establishing regular daily activities. If the target behavior is less frequent (such as weekly) or irregular, you may want to draw up a specific contract. Washing the car is one example. Cleaning their bedroom at the weekend is another. Contracts are very simple. You simply write out on paper what the required behavior is, what will happen if the children do it and what will happen if they do not do it. Since you will usually be looking at larger or more complex tasks, you will want to spell out just what is or is not acceptable. What, for example, counts as a tidy room? Toys put away, or just thrown in a box, or under the bed? Bed made? Carpet vacuumed? Obviously, your expectations will depend on the age and abilities of the child. But you must specify what you mean at the beginning, otherwise you will have these kinds of conversations:

'Mom, I'm done!'

96   *The GOOD CHILD Guide*

'Let me see . . . Well, what is all this stuff doing under the bed?'

'Well, it's out of sight, isn't it?'

'Not good enough.'

'What do you mean, 'not good enough'? The contract just says neat and tidy. Well, it is.'

'No it's not. Now finish the job!'

'Why should I? I did what it said. I'm out of here, and you owe me.'

Clearly these two have a different understanding of what 'neat and tidy' means.

As with charting, once you have drawn up the contract, you must stick to your end of it. The same rules apply.

Pocket Money

There are two types of pocket money: that which is earned, and that which is an unearned privilege. The two can be added together so that the weekly sum is partly earned and partly unearned.

The unearned pocket money is what you chose to give them because you feel they ought to have some money of their own. Since it is unearned, you are free to dock it if they have committed some crime. The earned money is of course dependent on them doing their chores, whatever they may be. If they fail to do them, then they lose out on the allowance. So this is another type of contract. It also means the same rules apply: if they earn it they get it, if they do not earn it they do not get it, and you keep quiet – no nagging and no shouting.

This can lead to some interesting outcomes on payday, depending on how the week has gone. Suppose that Ann gets $5 a week – half unearned, and the other half earned. This is what may happen:

1. Great week, chores done, good behavior. Ann gets the full $5.

2. Not so good. Chores done, but deliberately broke her sister's toy: Gets $2.50 for her chores (she earned it so you cannot remove it), but no more, as she needs to pay back her sister.

3. Average behavior, but only did some of the chores. Ann gets $2.50 unearned, and $1.25 for the chores she did do (in accordance with the agreed contract).

4. What a disaster. Really obnoxious behavior to a visitor, and only did half the chores: $1 earned, but you feel that she really does not deserve any of the unearned pocket money. But still you stay calm. And remember, tomorrow is a new day and a new week.

Dr. Noel Swanson

CHAPTER 4 - 4

Payment

There are times when you would really like your children to do something for you. It is not a regular responsibility, nor is it on a chart or in a contract. It is also quite clearly for your benefit, not the children's. A special visit to Auntie May's might be one such example: you do not want to be embarrassed by the children playing up, so you secure their good behavior with the offer of a payment.

Payments are a normal and appropriate way to deal with these situations. Your children are not your slaves. They do not have to attend to your every whim and fancy, although they should be reasonably helpful and co-operative about the home.

The distinction here is between the ordinary helping-out at home, like helping to carry in the shopping, and unusual or large jobs. The former are part of the informal give and take of life and will increasingly start to happen as you practice your praise and compliments. The latter might include jobs such as clearing out the garage or garden shed, moving the furniture out of the living room so that you can redecorate, washing the car and mowing the lawn. These are all 'grown-up' jobs that have little interest for, or relevance to, children, yet require quite a bit of work and effort to undertake.

If you want these big jobs done, you are going to have to pay for it. There are two ways you can do this. You can either ask for a favor, in which case you are making a withdrawal from your emotional account, or you can pay them, either with money or with a special treat or privilege. In either case, you are respecting their individual identity by giving them the option to say no. If you show respect, you will earn respect, so this will benefit you in the long run. Obviously, you cannot ask for too many favors, or you will go into overdraft again, and all your good work will be undermined.

Offering to pay someone for a job is essentially a one-off contract. The same rules apply. Once they earn it they get it. You cannot then confiscate it because afterwards they got into a fight.

98   *The GOOD CHILD Guide*

CHAPTER 4 - 5

Make it a Game!

Life does not have to be boring and serious all the time. One of the goals is to start having FUN again, remember? Well, let's apply that to getting good behavior started.

The make-it-a-game tactic is used for short behaviors that you used to nag them to do: getting ready for bed, putting their socks on, putting their clothes away. If they are regular tasks, then you might alternatively use Charting. It depends how serious the problem is. Or you can use this tactic for the less important behaviors that did not fit on the chart. Once again it is the emotion that counts: with charting you replace RTP mode with neutral. In this case you replace it with comedy mode. It is much less stressful than ranting and raving!

The most common way to do this is to set up a competition or race, either against the clock, against Mom or Dad, against brother or sister (take care with that one – we do not want to provoke a fight), or even against an imaginary child across the other side of town.

What happens if the child fails? First of all, you try to not let him fail. Set a reasonable target that he can achieve. If you are counting, vary the speed of your counting so that he achieves success just before you reach your goal. It makes him feel good. But you cannot let him win every time or he will start to manipulate you. So occasionally he fails to get done on time. What then? This is not the time for time-out or other punishments. The goal here is to have fun, to play a game. Sometimes when you play a game you lose. But it should still be fun. The same applies here. So what happens then? You tickle him so hard he begs for mercy! Or you hold him upside down by his ankles and pretend to smack his bottom. Anything, in fact, that produces lots of giggles.

Here are some examples:

Making it a Game 1: race against the count.

'OK, pyjama time. Quickly, before the giant gets you! One . . .' Dad starts counting at about three-second intervals, 'two . . .'

'Aaaagh, quick, Ben, the giant's coming.'

'What are you counting to?' asks Ben.

'Fifteen,' Dad replies. 'Three . . . four . . .'

Dr. Noel Swanson

99

Squeals of delight as the children rush up stairs.

'Ten . . . eleven. Fee, Fi, Fo, Fum! Twelve. Hope you are all ready – he's on his way!'
Dad starts to slowly pound up the stairs.

'Help!' the children scream.

'Thirteen . . . I smell the blood of an Englishman. Fourteen . . . Fift–'

'Stop! I'm done! I'm done!' they both cry out.

'Phew, that was close. He almost got you then. Well done, boys! Right, let's read a story
now.'

Making it a Game 2: Race against each other

This is the same game that children often play amongst themselves.

'OK, last one to get her coat on gets tickled!' Or is a banana, or a hairy monster, but
definitely not stupid, or indeed anything that might be a sensitive subject for your
particular child. We are having fun, remember, not trying to put people down and make
them feel bad.

Making it a Game 3: Race against the neighbor

This works well with younger children. You pretend that you have magic powers, and you
can see some other child (perhaps one of your child's friends) doing the same task in her
own house. You then make a race out of who will finish first.

'Come on, Trina, time to get up and dressed. Cathy is already out of bed, you know.'

'How do you know?'

'Ah, I've got magic powers. I can see her. She is just taking her top off. Tell you what,
let's see if we can beat her! . . . Oh, now she is getting her bottoms off! Quickly . . . Here,
I'll give you a hand.'

Since Trina is young, she may well need a bit of a hand getting dressed. Also, by doing
this you join in with the game as well. This way it is you and her together against Cathy,
which is much better than you against Trina.

'Oh, now she's pulling on her socks . . . left . . . Where are your socks? Quick.'

As Trina gets her clothes on, you give a commentary on how Cathy is doing. Strangely,
Cathy always seems to be just ahead. Until the end, that is:

'She's just putting her shirt on,' Mom says, just as Trina is about to get her shirt on, 'left
arm . . .' It's neck and neck. 'Right arm . . . now it's over her h–'

'Done!' shouts Trina with delight.

'Hey! You beat her! Well done!'

The task is done, you have had fun, Trina has had your undivided attention, you have spent quality time together. What more could you ask for?

CHAPTER 4 - 6

Praise and Compliments

I have put this at the end of this section because people tend to remember the end of a book more than the beginning, and this is important. If there is only one thing that you remember from this manual, let it be this section.

The charts, contracts, and the other Start tactics all work well and will help you to get your house in order. They will certainly help you to cut down on your shouting and nagging and the children's arguing and non-compliance. But in themselves, they will not make a happy home. It would be a bit like going to work at a job you do not enjoy. You know you have to do it because you need the money, but you really would rather be somewhere else.

The charts help to get you out of punishment mode. But you do not want to stay in neutral, you want to start having fun together as a family. You want the children to be happy, to gain in self-esteem and confidence, and to be a pleasure to have around.

This is where the good old-fashioned praises and compliments come in. They seem to have somewhat gone out of fashion these days. Instead, we (men especially) use our sarcastic humor to make an insult serve as a compliment. 'How you doing, you fat old pig?' translates into 'You are looking well!' Perhaps we are afraid that we would seem too forward or too emotional if we said what we meant straight out. But you cannot do that with children. They don't get it.

Hopefully, you have been practicing with some of the sample compliments on page 45. Now is the time to redouble your efforts. See how many kind things you can say this week. Do not restrict yourself just to the children. Tell your partner, your friends, your colleagues at work, even your boss. Work hard at it for a week and see what happens. I suggest that you put one of your star stickers on the face of your watch. Then every time you look at your watch, you will be reminded to pay a compliment to someone. Don't just sit there nodding, 'That's a good idea'. Put the manual down and go and do it now, before you forget.

How do you pay a genuine compliment?

First, find something genuinely good about someone – something that is based not on what they are, but on what they have done, something that is under their control. Be careful with this one – it is easy to get it wrong. Most young children, for example, do not buy their own clothes. Therefore, if you say, 'Nice shirt!' you are actually complimenting the girl's mother, who chose the shirt, rather than the child. Much better to say, 'You

102   *The GOOD CHILD Guide*

picked a nice shirt to wear today. The colors suit you.' Now you are complimenting her dress sense, as she could have chosen to put on the scruffy sweatshirt that is covered in grass stains. Similarly, 'You are a pretty girl' compliments her genes and does little to build up her confidence. More likely, it will make her vain, and teach her to value beauty and appearance more than a person's character and effort. Much better to say, 'I really like the way you did your hair today.' Even a plain girl can earn that compliment.

Having picked something to compliment, say something that specifically identifies what they have done and what you think about it. Here is an example:

'Thank you for helping to carry the shopping in. You saved me some time, and I enjoyed your company.'

Gradually, in time, you will find that your children will start to imitate you. That is, after all, how they learn best. After a while you may even start receiving some compliments yourself from friends and neighbors: 'My, what polite little children you have!' (Not a well-constructed compliment, but you will interpret it to mean, 'What a good job you have done in raising your children to have such good manners'.)

With time, you will see more and more good behaviors from the children – because they feel better about themselves, you, and the family, and because they like getting the compliments. This does not happen overnight, which is why you start off with the more formal methods. When it does, then you will be able to dispense with the charts and contracts. Until you start slipping back again, that is.

Special Treats and Rewards

Occasionally, you will feel particularly pleased with your children. Perhaps they have done you some big favors, or have really worked hard at some chores, or done really well at school. Or maybe you just want to celebrate the fact that you are a family together, or that you were given a pay rise at work. These are the times for special treats and celebrations.

The idea about special treats is that they are an unexpected bonus. It is a bit like your boss coming into the office and saying, 'This month has been outstanding. Well done, team. You have all worked hard and diligently to achieve this, so to celebrate we have decided to give you all an extra week's pay as a bonus!'. How well do you think that would go down among your colleagues? Children are the same. Special treats make them feel valued and important and help to strengthen the bonds between you all.

But it is important to remember that special treats are occasional. If they happen too often, they no longer seem special. They start to be viewed as rights, rather than privileges.

'Dad, are we going to the pictures this weekend?'

'Not this week.'

Dr. Noel Swanson

'Aw, why not? We went the last three weeks.'

'Those were special treats.'

'So? Why can't we go this week?' [And the whining starts.]

'That's one.' [Dad sensibly starts to count, rather than get sucked into an argument.]

But what a shame. Instead of the treats being special, they have become ordinary, and the children now feel that they are being deprived of something that is theirs by right.

Sometimes you will hear parents complain, 'I don't know why they whine so much, they get everything that they ask for!' That, of course, is exactly why they whine. Getting everything they ask for has become the norm, not a treat. So if they are not getting it, they then feel they are being unfairly deprived of their rights. So they whine. After all, it usually works.

Also, special treats are unearned. Suppose you say, 'I want you girls to be ultra-polite and well behaved when we visit Auntie May this afternoon. Then, if you have been good, as a special treat we will have a take-away tonight.' In this case, the treat is not unearned; it is dependent on their behavior. That makes this a contract, not a special treat, which means that you had better keep your end of the bargain if they keep theirs. That does not make it wrong – just recognize it for what it is.

104   *The GOOD CHILD Guide*

CHAPTER 5

SPECIFIC PROBLEM BEHAVIORS

CHAPTER 5 - 1

How to Analyze a Specific Behavior

Hopefully by now you are well on your way to a happier and more peaceful home. But there may be some specific behaviors that are still causing you problems. In this section we will look at how to analyze the problem behavior so that you can devise a strategy to change it. Then, in the following sections we shall apply these strategies to some common behavioral problems. If you have read the previous chapters, you already know the principles; it is now just a matter of applying them. If you have jumped straight to this section and have not read the earlier chapters, please do so now. Do not attempt to work through this chapter until you have done so.

You will already know that the bottom-line reason that your child is doing what he does is because it works. That is to say, the external motivators plus the internal modifiers plus the gambling odds make this behavior a better bet than an alternative behavior.

Your mission, should you choose to accept it, is to find out which of these factors you are able to change, what alternative behaviors you would like to encourage, and whether it is going to be worth the effort involved. So here goes. Follow this process through step by step and you should get there.

1)   Define the problem.

What exactly is it that your child is or is not doing? I recommend actually writing down a description of the problem behaviors. Be specific. Describe when it does or does not happen. Also describe the exceptions – when things have gone well. Describe what leads up to the behavior, what seems to set the scene or trigger it off, and also what happens after the behavior. Include in this account what you and others do in response. This may give you some clues as to what is reinforcing the behavior.

If you are unable to do this, or if your description is rather vague, particularly if you are using words like 'always' or 'never', then there are two probabilities that you need to look into. The first is that you are being overcritical. If you remain in a negative frame of mind where your child can do nothing right, then all your attempts at behavior modification are doomed to failure.

Alternatively, you may be describing a general attitude of non-compliance, defiance, and/or rudeness. This would suggest that your child is 'not a happy camper', and that it is the internal factors (e.g. mood) that are largely defining his behaviors. Probably included among them is your emotional bank account being heavily overdrawn.

Dr. Noel Swanson

107

Read Chapter 1 again. Work on making some deposits into the account: be polite, respectful, non-judgmental and complimentary, even in the face of ongoing insults. Spend time playing with your child, doing what she values, not what you think she ought to value. It will take time to turn it around, but it will not start until you start.

But maybe I do you a disservice. Perhaps you are already doing all this. At the same time, therefore, also look for other possible reasons for the poor self-esteem and anger – problems at school, with friends, with neighbors, with abuse. It may take some detective work, but if you genuinely show that you are on your child's side, and are prepared to fully listen, then you should eventually find out what is going on. If not, then it is probably time to seek professional help.

If the problem is a more specific and well-defined behavior, move on to the next stage.

2)   Is it a phase or a developmental stage?

It is no use complaining that your baby puts everything in his mouth. That is what babies do. Similarly, young children go through various behavioral and developmental phases. In infant school, for example, they get into the 'toilet jokes' phase. They love to make jokes about 'poo' and 'wee' and will delight in calling each other 'poo face'. You may not think it funny, but it will pass. Making a big fuss about it will only make things worse. The same applies to the many other phases kids pass through. You can check with other parents to see if their children are in the same phase as yours.

Also common among primary-school-aged children are tics. Often called 'nervous twitches' they include such things as eye blinking, shrugging shoulders, twisting or stretching the neck, and jerky movements of limbs or head. These are called 'motor tics' and are repetitive, *involuntary* movements that can occur at any time during the day, but often become more frequent at times of stress and when watching television.

Children can also get 'vocal tics'. Like motor tics, these are involuntary. Common ones are repetitive sniffing and snorting, grunting, coughing and humming. Rarely, they may involve more complex sounds or even whole words or phrases (as is the case with Tourette's syndrome, the 'swearing disease'). Tics can start at any age, but are most common among seven to nine year olds. They tend to wax and wane and may disappear completely for a while, only to come back as a different tic a few months later.

Tics are not dangerous, and rarely cause any problems to the child. But they can be irritating to parents. If you find yourself constantly telling your child : 'Stop snorting. Go get a hankie', it may be that he is lazy, it may be that he has a sinus problem or hay fever, or it may be that he has a vocal tic. If it is the sinuses, get it sorted out. If it is a tic, stop bugging him – it will not help. Since stress can make tics worse, it may be worth checking if there are any particular stresses in your child's life that you could help her to deal with.

3)   Why is it a problem?

If the behavior is dangerous, aggressive, immoral, or shows serious lack of responsibility, then clearly something needs to be done. If it is very irritating and is upsetting everyone else, then you will want to try to change it. But often the problem has more to do with our own agendas than with the child having a genuine problem.

Hole-digging Charlie is one such example. Charlie wants to dig holes. His Dad wants to plant flowers. Who is to say which is more important? Who has first rights over what to do with the garden? Digging holes is not dangerous, nor immoral, nor irresponsible. It is probably a phase that will pass in time. Perhaps a solution can be found by dividing the garden into Dad's area for flowers, and Charlie's area for holes.

Similarly, some children are loners. That is their personality and temperament. Such children like to stay quietly in their rooms reading, rather than go out and about socializing. Is it wrong? Is it dangerous? Or is it just that you are worried your child will never have any friends when she grows up? Perhaps she does not want a lot of friends and enjoys her own company. Some adults are like that and are quite happy with it. If that is the case, then leave her alone.

On the other hand, it may be that she is sad and lonely and does not know how to make friends. In that case, you will want to open up lines of communication with her, so that together you can start to work on the problem. Most likely you will do this by setting up structured play times with just one child at a time, so as to not overwhelm her. What you do not want to do is boss her about and tell her to come and play with the horde of noisy cousins that has just arrived.

Set realistic expectations. If they are too high, you will frustrate your children and burn yourself out.

4)   What type of problem?

Is it something you are trying to Stop, or something you are trying to Start? Bear in mind that often the easiest way to stop one behavior is to start another, usually opposite one. If you have been working on a 'Stop' behavior for a while and nothing is happening, it means that the rewards for doing it still seem greater than the punishments, or the rewards for doing the opposite. Check the following:

1.   Are you inadvertently rewarding the behavior, for example, by giving it lots of attention?

2.   Are you back in RTP mode?

3.   Do you sometimes give in and give them what they want?

4.   Are they angry or resentful, and therefore deliberately trying to get at you?

5.   Are they physically or mentally capable of stopping? Tics are an example, breaking things through clumsiness and poor co-ordination may be another.

6.   What else can they do that will get them the same attention or other rewards?

7.   Are the punishments appropriate and logical, or excessively harsh?

8.   Are there praises and compliments when they do get it right?

If it is a 'Start' behavior that is not happening, check these factors:

1.   Are there sufficient rewards in place, and do they get them when they have earned them?

2.   Can they get the same or similar rewards without having to work? Do you give in and let them watch their special program, even though they have not earned it? Or do they have so many unearned privileges that they really do not need the earned ones?

3.   Are the targets realistic? Do they have a fair chance of succeeding, or are they being set up to fail? If they are at two out of ten, aim, in the first step, to get to three, not nine.

4.   Is there an optimistic attitude, with plenty of praises and compliments whenever possible?

5.   Having set up the program, are you letting them get on with it? Or are you back in RTP or nag mode?

If it is a responsibility issue, are you allowing them to fail and live with the consequences, or are you still stepping in to make sure they do it? In this case it is you that is taking responsibility for the behavior rather than the child. This is seen very clearly in the next section.

Still Stuck?

If you have checked and rectified all the above, you should be back on track to success. If you are still stuck, then it is probably time to get some outside help. It may be that there is some serious medical or mental-health disorder. However, you will be surprised how quickly you can turn around even severe behavioral problems if you diligently follow these strategies. When parents complain that it is not working for them, by far and away the most common reason is that they are still too critical, have too high expectations, and are doing too much talking (and shouting). I see this happen all the time.

CHAPTER 5 - 2

Mornings

Mornings are often difficult times. The alarm goes off at 7 a.m., and everyone has to be out of the door by 8.30 a.m. Between these times the children have to get up, get dressed, wash their faces, clean their teeth, comb their hair, have breakfast, organize their bags, find their shoes, put on their coats, and get out of the door. Phew! What a rush.

When they were toddlers going to play school, you did most of it for them. As adults, they will need to do it themselves. No boss is going to be phoning them up every morning to tell them to get out of bed and get to work on time. Sometime in between there is a transition. This is where the frustration usually sets in.

Getting up and out in the morning is a responsibility. If you do not do it, there are natural consequences. As an adult, it is entirely your own responsibility – you are the one who has to live with the consequences, such as getting fired, including the fact that your actions may also affect others. When your children were infants, you took the responsibility for them, making sure they were where they should be at the right time. But children learn responsibility by having it. As long as you continue to do it for them, they will not learn for themselves. Gradually, this will lead to conversations like this one.

'Come on, Claire, it's time to get up!' Mother urges.

'Uhhhhh . . .'

Ten minutes later.

'Claire, breakfast in ten minutes. Get up! Now!'

Silence.

Another ten minutes. No Claire. Mother stomps upstairs, only to find Claire still in her pyjamas, reading her comics.

'Breakfast is now, young lady!' Mother snatches the comic away.

'Hey! I was reading that!'

'Not now, you're not. Now get moving or you will be late.'

And on it goes . . .

Dr. Noel Swanson

111

Half an hour later, Claire has finally had some breakfast and is now messing about in the bathroom:

'Claire, it is 8.30 a.m., time to go. Where are you?'

'Coming!' Claire replies, as she scampers down the stairs.

'Where is your school bag?' mother asks, with a groan.

'I don't know. I thought you had it! Did you put my lunch in?'

'Oh, for goodness sake, girl. Go and get your bag. Your lunch is in the fridge. It's your responsibility to get organized for school, you know!'

Is it? Sounds more like mother is taking the responsibility. Her fear is, of course, that if she did not nag and chase after Claire, then Claire would still be lying in bed. After all, it is the mother's responsibility to get her to school on time, isn't it?

At age three it is. At eighteen it is not. In between, it is in between. How much you make it their responsibility is up to you. Since this is a straightforward responsibility issue, you simply stop your nagging, and let her get on with it. Then you make sure that the natural consequences take their place. There are a couple of ways that you can do this.

1. Decide when they need to be out of the door in order to be at school on time, whether you are driving them, they are walking, or someone is picking them up. At that time, and not a minute later, you push them out of the door. If they are still in their pyjamas, too bad. If they have not finished their breakfast, never mind. If they have left their bag unpacked, they can explain that to their teacher. They then go to school partially ready, or alternatively, you throw their clothes outside with them. They can then get dressed on the doorstep or in the car.

    You are probably thinking, 'I couldn't possibly do that to my little angel.' Your little angel knows that, which is why she does not get going! Don't worry, you will only have to do it once.

    If you do end up sending her to school missing some clothes, give the school a call to let them know what is happening. I remember one lad who went to school without his shoes on, because he was messing about instead of getting ready. The teachers were wonderful. They completely ignored that fact, and let him spend the whole day at school shoeless. The next day he was ready on time.

    Incidentally, the same applies if they forget a particular item. Another boy I knew (aged seven) forgot to put his school shirt on. He still had his pyjama top on and then put his sweater on over the top. In actual fact, his parents did not notice, and so were as surprised as he was to discover, later on, that he was in school with his pyjama top instead of a shirt. He has not been so forgetful since then.

112   *The GOOD CHILD Guide*

2.   The alternative is to simply let them be late. Despite what you might think and what they say, most children want to be at school and want to be there on time. So let them be late if they are disorganized. But do not then give them a late breakfast. If they missed it, they missed it. Also, leave it to the child to explain to the teachers why he was late, and take the punishment for it if there is one.

This second method is more suited to the older child, or teen, and is probably not as quickly effective as the first. Of course, if the child chooses to miss school completely, there needs to be a logical consequence for that. See the next section.

CHAPTER 5 - 3

School Refusal And Separation Anxiety

Some children do not want to go to school. There are various reasons, but the bottom line is that going to school is less gain and more pain than not going to school. There are two main scenarios. The first is that there is something at school, or on the way to school, that is causing them anxiety or distress. This is sometimes called school phobia. The second is that leaving home, i.e. separating from parents, causes distress. This is usually called separation anxiety.

If your child has been regularly and happily attending school, and then suddenly does not want to go, or starts developing vague tummy aches and headaches for which he wants to stay off sick, the problem is most likely to be a school phobia. The clue is the sudden onset, with previously normal behavior. It suggests that something has happened which is upsetting your child. Perhaps a bully is picking on him. Or perhaps he is struggling with a subject and is afraid of failing, but also afraid of asking the teacher for help. Or maybe he is in trouble for something and wants to avoid the consequences. There may be a host of reasons, and your job is to get alongside him and try to sort it out with him and for him.

The more usual pattern is that there has been a long history of erratic school attendance. Often there are frequent absences for vague physical illnesses. This is especially common among children who were weak and sickly as babies and infants. These children get used to being 'sick' and all the privileges that go with it – especially the extra attention. Their parents also get used to them being sick and therefore are not surprised if they are sick again.

When it comes to leaving mother to go to school, these children get quite anxious and clingy, and may make a big fuss. If, as a result, mother stays, or the child gets to miss school, guess what? The behavior worked and so will be repeated next time. If, however, they are left at school, the anxiety often dies away pretty quickly.

Because they get anxious, these children do get headaches and tummy aches (which are the child's equivalent of an adult's headache). If, as a result, they miss school and get more attention, this pattern of behaviors gets reinforced. Over the years this can develop so that they end up spending hardly any time in school. Sometimes they get 'ill' during the day and have to come home from school early.

Whatever the root cause, the treatment is the same.

Every time they miss school, they get a concerned parent looking after them with much attention. Sometimes the parent even has to come home from work especially. What

114   *The GOOD CHILD Guide*

power! The basic principle, therefore, is to stop the rewards for not going to school, and add some rewards for going.

1. Check that there is no identifiable problem at school, or on the way to school. If there is, sort it out.

2. Check that there is no genuine, ongoing physical illness that requires bed rest.

3. Make a straightforward rule that he goes to school unless he is infectious (which means he has come out in spots), or has a measurable fever, which you check with a thermometer.

4. If he is not sick, he goes to school, in his pyjamas if necessary (see the previous section). Give him lots of praise and compliments when he does make it to school. But you probably do not need to physically force him out, as you can use the alternative to do its work:

5. If he does not go to school it must be because he is sick. So it is straight to bed, curtains drawn, lights off, and no television or computer games. He needs to rest and get some sleep. Also, he needs to drink plenty of fluids, so put a big jug of water next to the bed with instructions to drink it up by lunchtime. He is not allowed out of bed, except to go to the toilet. And you do not keep him company. Get on with your own work, and leave him to get bored. Come up with a small plate of sandwiches for lunch. If he is better, he can get up and go to school. If not, then leave him in peace again. Keep it up through the evening also. Before too long he will be begging you to let him get up so he can go to school.

Stay calm throughout all of this. Shouting or nagging will not get him to school any quicker; it will probably make it worse. But be firm and do not give in.

School refusal needs to be treated early and firmly. If left to go on for too long, it can become extremely entrenched, making it difficult, and sometimes impossible, to treat effectively. If you do not get a rapid response to your interventions, seek some professional help.

Dr. Noel Swanson

CHAPTER 5 - 4

Homework

Getting kids to do homework can be a major headache. Of course it is. By now, you will be able to spot the problem straight away! It is that word "getting". You will not be *getting* your kids to do anything. They will do it when they want to do it. Your job is to set things up so that they do want to do it.

Homework is an ideal candidate for Charting (page 90) or for a specific contract (page 96). Before you start that, however, you may want to consider the following points.

For many, if not most, children, homework is not very exciting. In fact, it may be quite boring. That is not a good start. Who wants to do something that is boring? This means that it is dependent on other, external, motivators if it is going to get done. It also means that it is quite susceptible to the internal de-motivators, like being tired and hungry after a long day at school.

The first thing to do, therefore, is to set up some sort of routine for homework. Decide with the children when the best time for doing it is. Probably they will want a snack first. It is usually a good idea to get it done straight away, before the television goes on, or before they go out to play. In the winter, with limited daylight hours, you may want them to play outside first, while it is still light, and then do the homework after supper. There is no right or wrong way, but try to make it consistent.

Decide also where the best place to work is. Is it the kitchen table, the living-room coffee table, their bedroom? Again, there is no right or wrong place, but the fewer distractions the better.

Often a regular routine, plus some incentive like watching a favorite TV program once they have finishcd is enough to get them going. Children who are struggling may need a little extra assistance. If they need a little help with the academic content, give it to them. But do not do it for them; it is their homework, not yours. Try to help them to succeed; nothing motivates as much as success. If they feel that homework is a grueling exercise in failure, they will soon find better things to do. If they are overwhelmed by it, divide it into smaller chunks and have a break in between – along with some praise and compliments, and maybe a cookie, to reward their effort so far. If the homework is consistently taking hours to complete despite their diligent efforts, it is time to talk to the teachers about it. If the child is behind in class, and finding the subjects difficult, she should not be punished by having to then struggle for hours with it at home.

116   *The GOOD CHILD Guide*

On the other hand, if the problem is not that they cannot do it, but that they will not, then it is an issue of responsibility (see Chapter 4). For the first few times, let the natural consequences take their course. Child and teacher can have their own conversation about why the homework did not get done. If it becomes a consistent problem, then it is time to haul out the chart, or draw up a contract. But do not forget to check if there are some internal modifiers at work to undermine your efforts (Chapter 1).

Finally, if your child has worked hard at her homework, be proud of her achievement. It is probably not perfect. No doubt you could do a better job. But being overly critical will destroy any hope of her taking pride in her own work. Instead, compliment her. Point out the bits that you like, or that she did well. Next time she will probably try even harder. In addition, you can ask her if she is happy with what she has produced. Being able to produce her own realistic assessment of her work, particularly with regard to how much effort she did or did not put into it, is even more useful to her than external compliments or criticisms.

CHAPTER 5 - 5

Bedtimes

It seems the two ends of the day are often the hardest for parents. The mornings, because there is an externally imposed time limit, and the evenings, because the parents want some peace and quiet and time for themselves. Incidentally, this is very much a northern European and North American custom. In Spain, children are regularly up late at night, as families do not even have their evening meals until 9 p.m. When they get to sleep I have not yet figured out, but I guess they fit it in somewhere.

The usual routine is that children do not want to go to bed. Not when so much fun can be had by getting the parents to run in circles around them. Normally there is some notional bedtime, but it is easy to stretch that out with requests like 'One more chapter', 'A glass of water please?', 'I'm hungry', 'I need to go to the toilet', 'I forgot to brush my teeth', and, of course, the best one of them all, 'I'm scared!' The more frustrated and harassed you get, the harder it is to get them to settle down.

Finally, you succeed. You sit down to read the paper. Five minutes later you hear footsteps coming down the stairs.

'What now?' you say.

'I've lost my teddy.'

'Honestly, can't I have any time to myself? I've already spent an hour getting you to bed, and now you're down here wanting me to find your teddy bear. Whatever next? Do you think . . .'

Oh, dear. Not a good scene.

What is rewarding the current behavior? From the child's perspective, it is a good gamble – he gets plenty of attention from the parents, and gets to stay up later. The down side? Occasionally you might really lose your temper and so they might get a smack.

If you want children to get to bed earlier and easier, there has to be a benefit in it for them. That means that you are going to have to put some effort into making it a positive experience for everyone. Trying to rush them off to bed will not work. Here are some suggestions:

Decide on the list of things that need to be done as part of the bedtime routine: getting tomorrow's clothes and bag ready, pyjamas, teeth, bath, story. Write them down and pin it up in their bedroom. Work out how long this list of tasks will realistically take them to complete. If it is going to take an hour, do not try to rush through it in half an hour. Resign yourself to putting aside anything else you wanted to do, and give your children this hour of your time. Then try to make this as hassle-free and fun as possible.

If lights-out is at 8 o'clock, and it is going to take an hour, then action time is 7 o'clock. At 7 o'clock you announce that it is bedtime. 'OK, folks! Time for bed! Last one in the bath is a hairy banana!' Turn off the television and computers. On some nights, you will make it a game. On others, you won't. Either way you do not get into nag mode. They have the list, you expect them to work through it. The carrot at the end is that you have until 8 p.m. to read stories, tell stories, chat, or just spend quiet time together. The sooner they are ready for bed, the sooner and longer they get the stories. Note the word quiet. The tickles are fine at the beginning, but the last half-hour needs to be a time to wind down. This is not the time for TV, the Game Boy, or any other high-stimulation activities.

Young children will need you to assist them with each step. Do not begrudge this; it counts as quality time, if you treat it right. Older children will be more independent, but they may still like to have you around. This hour is for them. Do not try to do your accounts or your letter writing at the same time.

When you finally get to 8 o'clock, the children will have had some good, peaceful time with one or other, or maybe both, of their parents. Now it is time for the lights to go off and the children to stay in bed. Be reasonable and leave a night light on, if they need one. But not a bright light – it keeps them awake and may tempt them to read. The rule is to stay quiet and to stay in bed. They do not have to go to sleep, as long as they are quiet. This pre-empts the 'I can't get to sleep!' cry. Normally, they would be allowed to get up and go to the toilet or to get themselves a drink, as long as it does not involve anyone else. But after 8 o'clock, you do not expect to hear from them again.

If you do hear from them again, you will need to respond in a way that is not going to reward their behavior. There are several options. One is to simply, but firmly, ignore it. If they are calling from their bed, wanting to tell you something, or asking you to do something, this can work. But you will need to tell them in advance, as you tuck them up, that you will ignore them if they shout. Otherwise they may panic, thinking that you have gone out and left them. As it is, it will get worse before it gets better. They will no doubt increase the volume in an attempt to rouse you from your well-earned rest to come and attend to their needs. This is a very powerful tactic if there are younger children who might be woken up by it. Ultimately they may come looking for you, which then forces you to deal with it in a different way.

Dr. Noel Swanson

An alternative is to start counting. Surprisingly, this is often quite effective, even though the ultimate penalty, when you get to 'three', is to send them to their rooms for time-out. Which is where they are already. Probably the reason it still works is that they have learned that when you start counting you mean business, so there is no point in pushing it. Even though there is not much of a penalty attached to it at this time of night, continuing to make a fuss is probably not going to pay off.

Some children are very persistent. Your counting does not impress them. They carry on shouting, or they come down to pay you a visit. They need to be firmly, but calmly, returned to their rooms. Do not engage in conversation – it only encourages them. If this is becoming a habit, it is time to invoke the power of a chart or contract to reward them for staying in bed (see Ben's chart, page 92).

If all else fails there are two more strategies:

1. Find yourself a comfortable chair and park yourself in it outside the bedroom door, along with a good book. Do not respond to calling out, and do not engage in conversation with them. If they attempt to leave the room, you calmly (very calmly) return them to bed. No talking, no emotion. Combine this with rewards for doing well. You will have to keep this up for some time, but if you are consistent, they will get the message. Incidentally, this is not the time to lock them in their room, as children will very easily get frightened and feel abandoned at night.

2. Use the paradoxical ('reverse psychology') approach. Tell your children that you have decided that since they want to spend more time up with the family, you are all going to play a game together. Then choose a boring game and play it over and over again, and keep playing it until they are begging for you to let them go to bed. Do this for several evenings. After that, when they start making a fuss at night, you can suggest to them that they stay up and play a game.

Finally, do not get tempted to take the easy way out and have them sleep with you in your room. You will only build up a habit that will be difficult to break and that you will regret for many a night. The only exception to this is when there is a violent storm outside. Treat this as a special, exciting event and allow them the privilege of sleeping on the floor next to your bed. Maybe even read them an extra story. By doing this you counteract their fears, and instead help them to associate storms with cosy warm evenings being battened down with the family they love.

Midnight Wakenings

All children wake several times during the night. So do you, come to that. Normal sleep consists of periods of deep sleep (so-called Stage 4 sleep) alternating with dreams (rapid-eye-movement, REM, sleep) and also shallow sleep, which often includes brief wakenings. Usually, you go straight back to sleep. But if there is some external stimulus, such as noise or light, or if your bladder is full, then you may wake up more fully and stay awake.

The trouble is that you can be trained to stay awake rather than go back to sleep. If children get attention during their brief wakening, this rewards staying awake. The result is that next time they will stay awake and seek attention (by crying or shouting), rather than go back to sleep.

To avoid this you need to ignore their wakenings as much as possible. If they stay in bed, do not go in to check on them. If you ignore them, they will probably go straight back to sleep. (This is especially true of babies – if you attend to their every cry, you will be training them to wake up regularly through the night.) If they start shouting and screaming , you will probably have to firmly tell them to be quiet, perhaps by counting. This is first of all to reassure them that you are there, and secondly to confirm that you still mean business. It is a bit of a bluff, really, because what are you going to do? Send them to their rooms for time-out? Even so, it seems to work.

If they do get up, your first assumption is that they need the toilet. Lead them there gently. They will often produce, even when they say they do not need to go. Do not turn the light on: you do not want to wake them up even more. Then lead them quietly back to bed. Hopefully, you can do all of this without them even waking up fully. With time, they will either learn to sleep through the night, or they will learn to take themselves to the toilet without your assistance.

The middle of the night is a difficult time. Everyone is at their lowest ebb, which makes for irritable and short-tempered parents. Resist it with all your strength. More than any other time, this is the time for peaceful restraint. It is hard, yes, but it pays off. The last thing that you want is uproar with the whole house awake. The more calmly you can handle it all, the quicker this phase should pass. Yet another of the joys of parenting.

Night Terrors, Nightmares, and Sleep Walking

Night terrors are common, harmless, but very frightening and upsetting for parents. All is quiet, with the children peacefully asleep. Suddenly, one of them sits bolt upright and screams at the top of his voice. Everyone wakes up in alarm! What is the matter, what has happened? You rush in to find him staring straight ahead, wide-eyed and still screaming. You try to comfort him, but nothing seems to work; he hardly seems to notice you are there. Eventually, he settles down and goes back to sleep.

Night terrors are common among pre-schoolers, but can persist through the primary-school years, sometimes occurring several times a week. They are a type of sleep disorder and, surprisingly, do not occur during dream (REM) sleep, but rather during Stage 4, the deepest stage of sleep. This is why you cannot get through to them – they are still deeply asleep, even though they look awake. Night terrors are not associated with frightening dreams and do not cause the child any harm. Eventually, they grow out of them. Although they are very distressing, and despite the fact that they wake up everyone else, the best thing to do is to ignore them. Do not wake the child up – it will take him longer to recover and to settle down again. Also, they will not remember anything, so there is no point in trying to ask them what they were dreaming about. It seems harsh, but the best thing to do is actually to buy some earplugs and try to sleep through it. In the morning they will have no memory of it.

Dr. Noel Swanson

The same applies to sleepwalking, which also occurs during Stage 4 sleep. Children have been known to do strange things in their sleep, including opening the front door and walking down the street. But waking them up is not the answer. Instead, make sure that they are safe – you may need to put in a stair gate, for example. If you happen to be awake while they are wandering about, gently lead them back to bed without waking them.

Nightmares, on the other hand, occur during dream (REM) sleep. Unlike the night terrors, the children do not scream, but often they cry out and clearly look like they are frightened or upset. On this occasion it is better to wake them. That ends the dream and allows you to comfort them. But try to avoid putting all the bright lights on. Be careful about asking them what the dream was about; it can be very easy to get them frightened again, although sometimes it can help to deflate the nightmare when they describe it in the light of day. Get them a drink, take them to the toilet, and sit with them for a while until they go back to sleep.

Early Mornings

Some children seem to be more like birds than humans – they seem biologically primed to wake up at 5 a.m. and then wake everyone else up with their own personal dawn chorus.

There is probably little that you can do to get them to sleep for longer in the morning. Obviously you will want to make sure that the room remains dark (put up some heavier curtains), and that there are no early-morning noises that might be waking them, such as the heating coming on. But some children just seem to need very little sleep.

If that is the case, one option is to put them to bed later. As with jet lag (which is actually what it is), it will take them a week or two to adjust to the new time schedule.

The other option is to train them to be quiet in the mornings. Here the goal is not to keep them asleep, but to allow them to wake up, and get up, but without waking everyone else in the process. This takes some preparation. First, you will need to discuss it in detail with them and hopefully negotiate some degree of co-operation. Then, what many parents have found to be helpful, is to put together a 'morning kit' that contains a number of quiet activities they can do when they wake up. If these are not available the rest of the day, then it makes them even more attractive in the morning. And, of course, add in some charting or a contract.

If they do make a noise, ignore it or remind them quietly, and once only, that they need to remain quiet if they want to earn their rewards. Since they did wake you up, they lose one of their 'quiet-in-the-morning' points, but they can still earn the rest if they remain quiet. Do not shout at them, even if you feel like it. Praise and compliment them when they do succeed in playing quietly.

122   *The GOOD CHILD Guide*

CHAPTER 5 - 6

I'm Bored!

Children have more toys and more organized entertainment than ever before. Yet they still complain of being bored. Perhaps the two are linked. If children are used to having every waking minute filled with activities, there will be an aching void if there happens to be five minutes spare with nothing to put in them. It is then that they come to you, expecting you to do something about it.

When they do, you can offer them a tremendous opportunity to learn some independence, self-reliance and creativity. Ignore their complaints. Do not reward their whining and complaining by organizing some entertainment for them. Let them do some problem solving for themselves. Once they get over the shock, you will be amazed at what they are able to come up with.

Incidentally, I strongly recommend that you do not resort to the electronic babysitters to keep them quiet. There is mounting evidence of the harm that is caused by too much time spent in front of the television and various computer games: they increase violence and aggression, as well as obesity and the risk of heart disease, discourage creativity and imagination, decrease school performance and social skills, and so on.

You do not have to ban TV completely. But restrict its use, for example by having it only available for limited periods earned on a chart, or only use it when you are watching together as a family. Then you can discuss what you are watching, often a good opportunity for talking about family values such as honesty. There are plenty of other things that children can do, rather than sitting passively in front of a screen.

One way to assist them is to create a list of things that they can do. If you can do this jointly with them, even better. Stick it on the fridge, next to the Deal. You will find a sample list on page 138 which you can customize for your own use. Then, when they complain that there is nothing to do, you can point them towards the list and say, pick one of those, or find something else to do, but stop complaining. You will note that option 52 on the list is to stay bored. They can do that if they want to; it is their choice. But if they come back at you again, complaining, then you say, 'That's one...'

Dr. Noel Swanson
123

CHAPTER 5 - 7

Attention Deficit Hyperactivity Disorder

Some children are placid, others are lively. A small number are positively hyperactive. These children are impulsive, disorganized, forgetful, loud, and easily frustrated, which often leads to some lively temper tantrums. These children are so hyperactive and impulsive that they are in trouble wherever they go. They just do not think before they do things, and they do not learn from experience or from applied discipline. These children have significant difficulty in fitting in with the normal expectations of home and school, both of which are usually just too stimulating for them. Since their problems with controlling their behaviors are so problematic, their condition has been described as a disorder. It has gone through a number of names over the decades, but the current one is Attention Deficit Hyperactivity Disorder (ADHD).

Obviously a full discussion of ADHD is outside the scope of this manual. Further information can be found in numerous books (check your library), from your doctor, school nurse, health visitor and local child mental health clinic.

There are two points that are worth making:

1.   If your child has ADHD, you did not cause it. ADHD definitely runs in families and has a large genetic component to it. In addition there are a number of environmental factors that may be involved. But it is extremely unlikely that bad parenting causes it. It is just one of those things that, for whatever the reason, you have been blessed with a challenging child instead of an easy one (see page22).

      Furthermore, because these children have such short attention spans, and are so impulsive, the severe ones do not respond well to even the most consistent behavioral program. In other words, if your children are at the moderate to severe end of the spectrum, then even your best efforts at putting this manual into practice may have only limited results. They will continue to do foolish, impulsive, actions that keep getting them into trouble. If that is the case in your family then it is time to seek some professional help.

2.   Even so, children with ADHD need this program even more than the less active ones. Because they are so easily distracted, they stand the best chance of controlling their behaviors if the discipline is highly structured, very immediate, and very consistent. So do not give up on them. Instead determine that you will work even harder at producing a calm, optimistic, reward-based environment. Then you will be giving them the best possible chance for success.

124   *The GOOD CHILD Guide*

No, it is not easy. Yes, you will often feel worn out and harassed. No, it is not fair, but then life isn't. Like the children we have discussed right through this manual, you have a choice in dealing with this unfair world: you can make the best of it, or you can complain and make a fuss. I hope, for your sanity as well as your children's, that you will choose the former. I am sure you will, otherwise you would not be reading this manual. You do not have to struggle alone, however. There are many more out there in the same position, some of whom have come together in parent support groups. Speak to your doctor or health visitor.

CHAPTER 6

AS TIME GOES BY

CHAPTER 6 - 1

How Are You Doing?

I had been seeing Catherine and her family for several months. When they first came to see me, life at home was pretty bad. The parents were having tremendous problems with Catherine's obnoxious and defiant behavior. Everyone was shouting at each other. Fun times were non-existent, and the parents were even talking about separating because of all the stress.

Over the weeks they worked hard at putting into place the strategies described in this manual. They learned to count instead of shouting. They looked hard, and found some behaviors that they could praise and reward. Gradually, things improved.

When they came in this time, I had not seen them for a couple of months and so was curious to find out how it was all going. They started by telling me how much calmer everything was now. But they were still having difficulties with bedtime.

'So, overall, how would you rate family life now?' I asked.

'Oh . . . about two out of ten, I guess,' Dad said.

'Really?' I was somewhat surprised at the low score, given how much better things were now than they had been. 'So, if you are at a two now, what were you at six months ago? I thought that at that time you had scored life at a two.'

'Oh, well . . . if we score it in on the same scale that we used then, I would say we are at about a nine now!' they both exclaimed.

Isn't it funny how perspectives change? I wonder which felt better, to score it at nine compared to two six months ago, or to score it at two compared with some new idealized scale? Sometimes it can be helpful to keep a log or a diary of behavior, so that you can remind yourselves how far you have come. Like Catherine's family, it is easy to get caught up in today's troubles and lose sight of the big picture.

The Family Meeting

One way to keep on track is to have a regular family conference. Initially, you might do this weekly (or even daily, if life is very stressful), but when things are going better you can reduce the frequency. Businesses, of course, do this as a matter of routine. Without a regular review, they would never know if they were meeting their targets or if their business was booming or about to go bust. Why should families be any different?

Dr. Noel Swanson

The purpose of a family conference is to ask some basic questions: 'How did we do this week? What did we do well? What do we need to improve upon?' Note the positive orientation: it is not 'What did we do wrong?' but 'What do we need to improve upon?' Some families find it helpful to rate the week out of ten. You could even plot a graph of your progress. Again, the purpose of this is to find the good things and build upon them. Even if you rated the week as one out of ten, that is still better than zero. Pick out the one thing that went well, and resolve to do it even better or more frequently.

The conference is also a forum at which people can raise concerns that they have. This is a time at which resentments can be sorted out, and irritations discussed. The idea is to prevent people from nursing resentments before they fester and grow, ultimately undermining the whole family.

The overall idea is that the family works together as a team to make life better for you all. The basic assumption is that you are on the same side. No business would survive if at every board meeting all the members spent the whole time criticizing and tearing each other apart. A house divided against itself will not stand. You, as the parents, must of course take the lead in showing how this is done. To help you, here are some rules for a family meeting:

1. Choose a regular time and a regular place to meet. You should meet around a table, as it promotes a more businesslike atmosphere. One parent should chair the meeting and keep order, the other should write a record of what was discussed and decided upon. In this way you can keep each other accountable for what you have all resolved to do.

2. Set an agenda. You will find a sample agenda on page 139.

3. Maintain a positive, problem-solving approach. No shouting, no insults, no accusations. If one person starts talking like this, then whoever notices it first should quietly stand up. This acts as a signal to halt the argument and get back into problem-solving mode. Other members should also quietly stand up, until those that are arguing get the message and apologize for disrupting the meeting. There is no distinction of age. If the parents do the shouting, then the children should stand up. When you stand up, stay silent, do not get embroiled in the argument. When peace is restored, sit down and continue the discussion.

   You may need to have one person acting as a mediator so that both sides can say their piece. Try to get each person to define what their problem is, not what the other person is doing wrong. Write it down if necessary. For example, 'My problem is that it upsets me when I have spent two hours cleaning the kitchen, to then turn around and find muddy footprints all over the floor. It makes me feel that no one appreciates the work I do.' This works much better than: 'I am fed up with you traipsing mud all over the floor every time I have just washed it.' Is it really every time? Don't skip over this part, as often the very process of accurately defining the problem will prompt people to come up with a solution.

You cannot change someone else, therefore problem solving works much better if you focus on yourself, i.e. the part that you have played in the conflict, rather than pointing out the faults of the other person. After all, all they will do then is point out your faults, so it gets you nowhere. Apologize when you are in the wrong (see the 6 As of Apology, at the end of this manual). That applies to parents too!

4. At the end, agree on something fun that you want to do as a family. Reward yourselves for the successes.

Slipping Back

It happens in every family. You start the program, and within weeks life is much calmer. After a while, you decide that you no longer need the charts or contracts. Occasionally, you miss a family conference because you were on holiday, or you had visitors. Gradually, you miss more and more, until you no longer have them at all. But life is still pretty good, so you are sure you can manage without them.

Six months later, everyone seems to be shouting at each other again! The children are not getting their chores done, and you are having to nag them to get going in the mornings.

What happened is you started slipping back again. Why? Probably because you are back in RTP mode, and you have forgotten the basic rules. Go back to the beginning, read the manual again to remind yourself, and then start following the program again. Before too long you should be back on track again.

Say What You Mean and Mean What You Say
- Cut The GAB
- Expect First Time Obedience
- Follow up with ACTION

They Are Getting Older

As children grow up, their abilities change. Not surprisingly, that means that your expectations also need to change along with them. The trick is to move at the same speed that they do: too fast, and you become overcritical because they do not match up to your high standards; too slow, and you become overprotective, preventing them from doing what they are well able to manage.

On the whole, you want to be on the lookout for ways to say yes to them. That is, to find ways to give them more responsibilities, and with it, more freedom. Instead of saying, 'No, you can't do that, you're too young', try saying, 'I would like to be able to say yes to that, but I do have some concerns about your safety and your ability to handle that responsibly. Let's see if there is a way to satisfy those concerns.'

One way might be for the child to earn the greater freedom by demonstrating his growing responsibility in another, linked area. You can use a contract for that. For example: 'I'll tell you what. You demonstrate to me that you can look after the hamster for three months, without me having to remind you to do it, then at the end, if you have succeeded, you can have a pet gorilla.' Or something along those lines.

On the other hand, if you find yourself telling the child off all the time, perhaps your expectations have run ahead of the child's abilities, Time to reset them, and get back into reward mode (see Chapter 2).

CHAPTER 6 - 2

Final Words

Being a parent is tough. It is a heavy responsibility – you have brought these little nippers into the world, and somehow you have to nurture and guide them until they are ready to spread their wings and take their full place in society.

Yet it should not be a burden. With some thought and effort, it can become the most fulfilling and enjoyable part of your life. The fact that you have made your way through this manual and got this far is a good start. You obviously number among those parents who love their children, and are willing to do what it takes to be the best parents that those children could have. That determination, plus the fact that you recognize you are not perfect and thus there are always improvements you can make, is already 90 per cent of the battle. Many do not even make it that far!

So, bon voyage! I hope that you have found this manual useful, and that you, and your family, have a more enjoyable journey through life as a result. Life will have its ups and downs, some caused by outside events, some caused by family members. But if you stick together, you will make it through. Remember, they really are little angels – God's gift to us to make our lives fuller and richer than if we just focused on our own needs and wants. So enjoy the ride. Don't forget to stop and smell the roses. Celebrate the fact that you are a family together! Have some FUN along the way.

CHAPTER 7

APPENDICES

These may be freely copied for your personal use

Suggestions for Rewards

Daily

Have a favorite/special dessert
Have a special snack
Have a favorite meal
Special TV privilege
Half hour on the computer
Half hour with a games console (e.g. Nintendo)
Hear an extra story at bedtime
Stay up for a later bedtime
Special "private time" with parent - own choice of activity
Tokens for general exchange for any of the items below

Weekly or Special Treats

Play a board game with the family
Rent a special video
Have a picnic for supper
Stay with grandparents
Have a friend home for supper or overnight
Prepare a special dinner with a parent for the whole family
Go on a special "cultural outing" (concert, film, museum)
Go on a special "sports outing" (bike ride, skating, swimming, canoeing)
Camp overnight in the backyard with Mom or Dad
On a weekend day, wear make-up or Mom's jewelry
Purchase of : CDs/tapes, sports equipment, furnishings for bedroom

Things to Do When You Are Bored

1   Play outside
2   Catch insects in the garden
3   Dig for worms
4   Climb a tree
5   Take the dog for a walk
6   Play football
7   Go to the park
8   Ride a bike
9   Rollerblade
10 Pull some weeds
11 Build a den
12 Go to the library
13 Play with Lego or K'nex
14 Make a kite
15 Build a model from a kit
16 Build a model from papiér maché
17 Paint Warhammer models
18 Set the table
19 Bake a cake
20 Tidy up bedroom
21 Read a book
22 Explore the encyclopedia
23 Do an experiment
24 Invite a friend over
25 Visit a friend
26 Do the doll's hair
27 Play house
28 Sew a soft toy
29 Learn cross stitch
30 Invent a gadget
31 Design a new game
32 Draw a picture
33 Invent a new language
34 Write a story or a book
35 Write a poem
36 Practice the piano

37 Do some homework
38 Practice handwriting
39 Make a present/card for parents
40 Play a game - monopoly
41   cards
42   dominoes
43   marbles
44 ....
45 ....
46 ....
47 ....
48 ....
49 ....
50 ....
51 ....
52 Stay bored

The GOOD CHILD Guide

Agenda for Family Conference

1. Review the week. Everyone scores the week out of ten, and says what went well and what they were happy with. This does not have to relate to family life only; school, work, and outside interests can also be discussed. Congratulate and compliment each other on what went well.

2. Talk about any problems or concerns that individuals had or are having, either in or outside the home. Remember it is the problem, not the person, that is the enemy. Do not make accusations or criticisms about another family member. For example, avoid, 'You did this ...' and 'You always ...' or 'You never...'

   Instead, use sentences that begin with I:
   'I was upset when this happened...'
   'I was very angry about...'
   'I am having a problem with things being left on the floor'.

   Apologize when you were in the wrong, or when you handled a situation badly, and ask for forgiveness. This promotes dialogue and will get the problem solved. Making accusations and damning statements will just provoke a row.

   Everyone else at the table has a responsibility to mediate this, and to stop the discussion if it is turning into an argument. Do this by standing up quietly. Do not sit down again until those that are arguing have stopped and are willing to start calm discussions again.

   Continue the discussion until, as a family, you have found a solution that will please everyone. When you do, write it down.

3. Decide, as a family, any goals or special plans for the coming week. Aim to have some fun together.

4. Once you close the meeting, do not reopen any of the potential arguments. If any were not fully resolved, call another meeting.

5. Obviously, anything discussed in the meeting is confidential, and not to be repeated to school friends or workmates. Respect each other's privacy.

Dr. Noel Swanson

The 6 A's of Apology

Admit

Admit what you did, without telling lies first, and without having to be asked.

Account

Explain what you were trying to do, or what you were thinking, even if you were just being careless and not thinking about it.

Acknowledge

Show that you are aware of the pain or hurt that you have caused the other person. Tell them that you wish that you had not caused these hurts, and that you are feeling bad yourself because of the hurt that you caused.

Affirm

Indicate that you still want the person to be your friend, to like you, and to forgive you. Ask the person to forgive you, and show that you want to improve your relationship with the person.

Amend

Make amends by doing something to make up for the pain you have caused. Do a favor, bring a gift, do chores for the person, or invite the person to do something fun with you. Explain that you want to repay the person for the hurt you have caused.

Adjust

Think about what you can do differently next time, so that you won't repeat the mistake. Change something to prevent it from happening again.

Example: *"I'm sorry I did that, it must have really hurt you. I still want to be your friend. Let me make it up to you. I would like to do this favor for you to show you that I am really sorry."*

(Note: I am indebted to the unknown author of this piece - if you can enlighten me on whom it was, I will be glad to give due credit in the next edition of this manual)

THE DEAL

Responsibility	Pts	Sat	Sun	Mon	Tues	Wed	Thu	Fri	Total
Daily Totals:									

Rewards	Pts. Needed

Notes and Definitions